THE ILLUSTRATED
TIBETAN
BOOK
OF
THE DEAD

THE ILLUSTRATED
TIBETAN
BOOK
OF
THE DEAD

STEPHEN HODGE *with*

MARTIN BOORD

A NEW TRANSLATION

with COMMENTARY

 A GODSFIELD BOOK

Library of Congress Cataloging-in-Publication Data available

10 9 8 7 6 5 4 3 2 1

First paperback edition published in 1999 by Sterling Publishing Company, Inc
387 Park Avenue South, New York, N.Y. 10016
© 1999 Godsfield Press
Text © 1999 Stephen Hodge and Martin Boord

Distributed in Canada by Sterling Publishing
c/o Canadian Manda Group, One Atlantic Avenue, Suite 105
Toronto, Ontario, Canada M6K 3E7
Distributed in Australia by Capricorn Link (Australia) Pty Ltd
P O. Box 6651, Baulkham Hills, Business Centre, NSW 2153, Australia

Printed and bound in China

Sterling ISBN 0-8069-7077-4 (Trade)
ISBN 0-8069-6431-6 (Paper)

CONTENTS

---- ❁ ----

INTRODUCTION
6

THE GREAT LIBERATION THROUGH HEARING
IN THE TRANSITIONAL PHASE OF DEATH
24

The Opening Phase
26

The Visions of the Reality Phase
42

The Transitional Phase of Rebirth
114

Glossary
138

Suggested Reading List
141

Useful Addresses
143

Acknowledgments
144

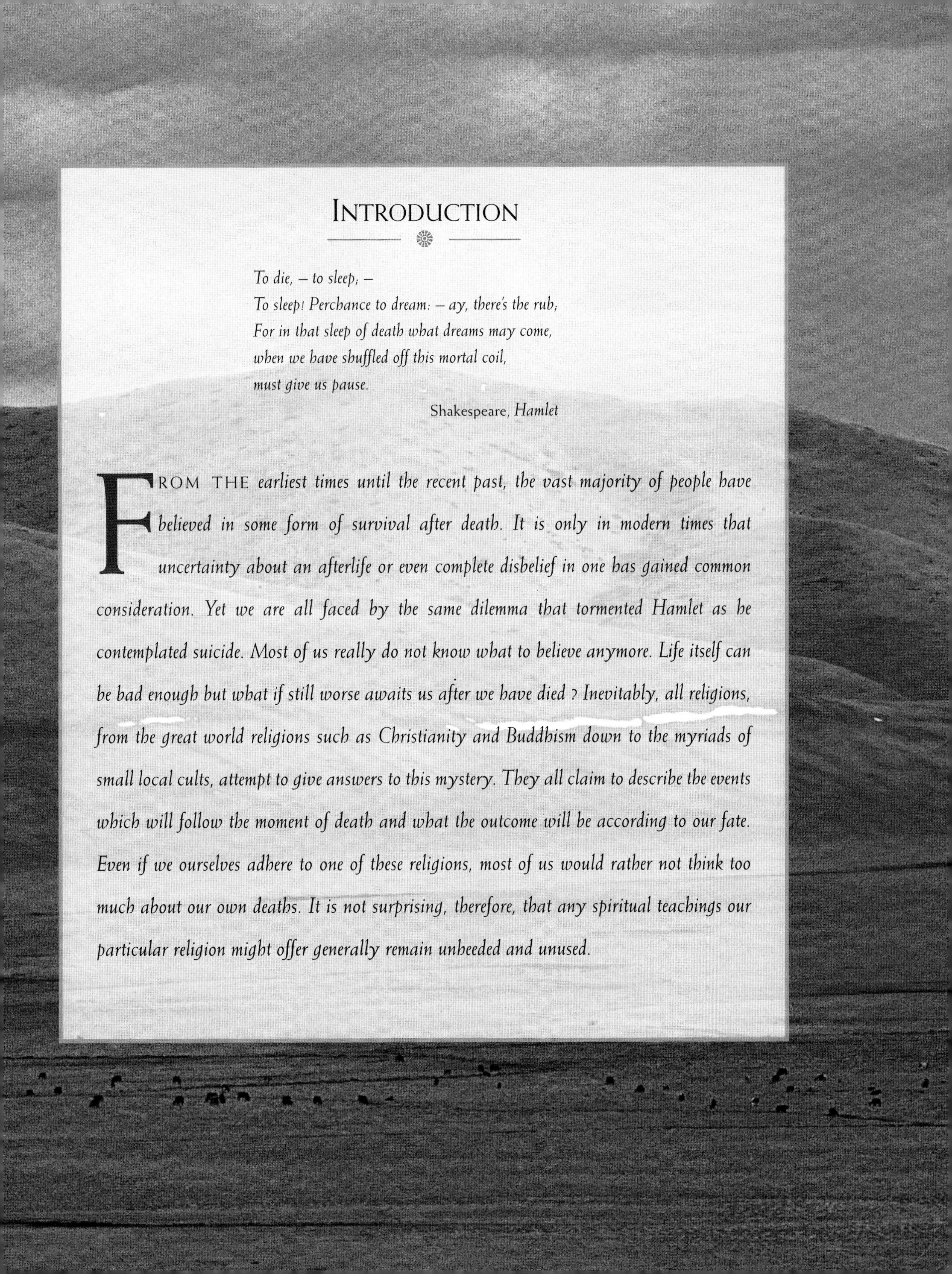

INTRODUCTION

✳

To die, – to sleep; –
To sleep! Perchance to dream: – ay, there's the rub;
For in that sleep of death what dreams may come,
when we have shuffled off this mortal coil,
must give us pause.

Shakespeare, *Hamlet*

ROM THE *earliest times until the recent past, the vast majority of people have believed in some form of survival after death. It is only in modern times that uncertainty about an afterlife or even complete disbelief in one has gained common consideration. Yet we are all faced by the same dilemma that tormented Hamlet as he contemplated suicide. Most of us really do not know what to believe anymore. Life itself can be bad enough but what if still worse awaits us after we have died? Inevitably, all religions, from the great world religions such as Christianity and Buddhism down to the myriads of small local cults, attempt to give answers to this mystery. They all claim to describe the events which will follow the moment of death and what the outcome will be according to our fate. Even if we ourselves adhere to one of these religions, most of us would rather not think too much about our own deaths. It is not surprising, therefore, that any spiritual teachings our particular religion might offer generally remain unheeded and unused.*

A MODERN SPIRITUAL CLASSIC

One set of teachings has defied this general trend and has attracted increasing attention and interest over the past fifty years or more. Although it has its roots in a culture alien to many people in the West today, it is perhaps its detail and seductive confidence that have served to make the so-called Tibetan Book of the Dead *a modern spiritual classic. This version of the* Tibetan Book of the Dead *is another attempt to make accessible the teachings and guidance offered by this tradition of Tibetan Buddhism. However, a deeper understanding of its underlying concepts will serve to make the work both more valuable and helpful for people in the West faced by death, whether their own or that of their loved ones.*

Perhaps the most important idea to bear in mind is the Tibetan Buddhist view of human nature and how it relates to that mode of freedom and wisdom called "enlightenment." Buddhism most emphatically stresses the centrality and primacy of the mind. The mind is the source of all things; it contains within it the possibility of enlightenment or else continued repetition of the dreary miserable round of lives in the cycle of existence. Indeed, it is the view of these teachings that the mind in its purest form, shorn of all ignorance and negativity, is inherently enlightened and replete with all the qualities one normally associates with enlightened beings such as the Buddhas. This pure primordial mind that precedes any manifestation of our own egocentric lives is said to be the very substance of reality.

Unfortunately, this primordial mind remains buried deep within our being for most of the time, unseen and unnoticed. Due to a dense overlay of spiritual ignorance, the various facets of enlightenment that are present in that mind, such as compassion, insight, tolerance and so forth, can only reveal themselves in a perverted and distorted manner. Thus, love becomes attachment and jealousy, compassion becomes hatred and anger, insight becomes opinionatedness and stupidity. These and other negative emotions then become the driving force for ever-greater egoism and spiritual poverty.

While Buddhism offers many techniques for eliminating this mass of negative tendencies and the sinful actions they give rise to, none are so powerful and direct as these teachings concerning the time of dying and death. Although at first reading this strange and wonderful book may seem confused and chaotic, in fact it reveals the way out of confusion and chaos. So it is said that, merely by hearing these instructions and taking them to heart, all people will be able to throw off painful uncertainty, will be empowered to replace the misery of the average human condition with a clear mind, at peace with itself and filled with understanding. In effect, the Tibetan Book of the Dead teaches us how to recognize our pure primordial mind and thereby to gain enlightenment. Hence, this book is addressed as much to the living as to the dead and dying. It is implicitly a book about life. It is a book about how to live, as well as a book about how to die.

THE TRANSITIONAL PHASE

From day to day, ordinary life is filled with beginnings and endings. As each moment passes, a new one appears to take its place. Waking up in the morning, we rise and go about our ordinary activities of washing, getting dressed, eating breakfast and so on. Nothing in life stands still. Movement and change are the very essence of life and yet our normal tendency is to believe that everything is fixed and solid. We wish to believe that all we see is real and secure, even though our ordinary experience tells us that nothing remains unchanged and nothing lasts forever. On the contrary, everything in the world around us is constantly falling apart and requires a great deal of maintenance on our part if we wish to hold it together. What happens during this process of change is the great mystery revealed in symbolic form within this book. The state called here "the transitional phase" (Tibetan: "bardo") is the actual moment

of change, occurring at the end of one phase and the beginning of the next. It is the state of flux itself, the only state that can really be called "real." It is a condition of great power and potential within which anything could happen. It is the moment between moments. It may seem to span an entire lifetime, like the moment between being born and dying, or it may be imperceptibly short and fleeting, like the moment between one thought and the next. Whatever its duration, however, it is a moment of great opportunity for those who perceive it. Anyone who can do this is called a yogin. Such a person has the power of destiny in their hands. He or she has no need of a priest to guide him towards the clear light of truth, for he sees already the clear light of truth in the inter- mediate phases that occur between all other states. Refusing to become trapped in the false belief that all about him is fixed and solid, the yogin moves with

calm and graceful ease through life, confident that changes are now under his own direction. He becomes

the master of change instead of its slave. To one who understands this and develops some skill in its appli-

cation, the difficult uncertainties of life become no more troublesome than the bardo of getting dressed in

the morning. Between waking up and getting dressed, one must decide what clothes to wear. That is all.

It should not be a problem. Similarly, between any encounter and one's reaction to it, there is an inter-

mediate space that offers choice to those who can see it. One is not obliged to react on the basis of habit

or prejudice. The opportunity for a fresh approach is always there in the intermediate state for those who

have learned to recognize it. Such recognition is the essential message of this ancient and profound book.

THE THREE JEWELS

In order that we might become a little more receptive to the teachings contained here, the Tibetan Book of the Dead, *being a Buddhist scripture, advises us to make offerings to the Three Jewels — the Buddha, his Teachings* (dharma), *and the Community of practitioners* (sangha). *Those who are not Buddhists should make offerings or prayers to whatever symbols of spiritual ideals their faith offers. However, the principle remains the same. By giving a little of ourselves at the start of the process, we automatically begin to loosen up and soften our hard-edged ideas concerning the fixed and solid world around us. Presenting offerings to the fully awakened Buddha who has realized the true nature of the human condition, we acknowledge the possibility of such awakening and prepare for that realization ourselves. By presenting offerings to the Truth realized and taught by the Buddha, we acknowledge its value in bringing meaning to our lives. Then, by presenting offerings to the community of those who have followed in the Buddha's footsteps, we seek their help in guiding us to that same level of understanding. We then call upon these Three Jewels to help us in our quest for liberation.*

THE SPACE BETWEEN THOUGHTS

Afterward, in a receptive state of mind, we strive through meditation to catch a glimpse of the clear light of the intermediate state as it presents itself while we sit. Observing the meaningless flow of thoughts that pass through the mind, one should try not to become involved. Just let them be. A thought that is ignored soon goes away. And there it is! The space between thoughts. How wonderful to see!

At first when we begin to practice, this small glimpse of reality quickly passes and the mind is again flooded with attractive thoughts that have us by the nose. Unable to resist their lure, we follow helplessly and are once more entangled in their snare until the whole train of ideas comes to some kind of conclusion. Then, suddenly, there it is again! That small gap between one thought and the next. That small gleam of clear light, utterly devoid of graspable form or content.

With practice, we can learn to see a great deal within the open space of this clear light, and then we begin to value it very highly. The clear, bright, calm space between moments of anxious concern is pervaded with a sense of joyous peace that is utterly refreshing. It seems to fill us with energy so that we become ready for anything and yet it does not seem to push in any direction, so that the choice of how to use the energy remains totally private and personal. The space simply presents us with a wonderful opportunity to break free from the negative thought-patterns and habitual behavior of the past. It is an intermediate state filled with freedom: the freedom to be the best that we can be without fear of restraint or censure, the freedom to live at peace with ourselves, in harmony with our own, true nature and in control of our own destiny.

If such rewards are gained in this life, there will be no need for anyone to read aloud these teachings at the time of our death. But for those who are not so skilled, the intermediate state between living and dying arises naturally as an important time in which such thoughts should be brought to mind. At that time, if a trusted friend of the dying person is available to explain clearly what is happening, that is good. Indeed, for those of no real attainment, the occasion of death can be a terrifying experience and it is most comforting and helpful to have a guide at hand to show a pathway through fear.

THE DISSOLUTION OF THE FIVE ELEMENTS

❉

The first sign of approaching death is the collapse of the five senses. The dying person may vomit and lose all desire for food. The body begins to grow cold and, fearful of falling down, he or she may be afraid to lift up the head. An experienced guide, recognizing this as the first sign, should strive to make the dying one comfortable with soft cushions and kind words. The guide should mark the dissolution of the bodily elements and, in a soft, clear voice should explain to the dying person that, as the external flesh begins to tighten and shrink, he or she feels heavy and experiences the sensation of falling from a great height because the element earth is now crumbling. As earth begins to dissolve into water, the shape of the body becomes loose and the muscles grow weak. The mind feels dull and hazy. As liquids begin to ooze from the mouth and nose, the dying person feels a burning sensation of thirst and this is because the element of water is now dissolving into fire. Then the mind begins to have momentary flashes of clear lucidity as the element of fire dissolves into air. The body temperature of the dying person drops right down and the eyes roll in the head, unable to recognize even the well-wishers and friends who are gathered at the bedside. As the element of air dissolves into space, breathing becomes difficult, the mind becomes agitated and the body twitches and shakes. As the breathing seems to cease altogether, one has a vision of hazy shapes like wisps of smoke which then disappear. Thus the elements are dissolved. In the case of sudden death by illness or accident, however, or when one dies far from home while on a journey in a foreign land, guidance may be difficult. It is better, therefore, for each person to be aware as far as possible of these signs of death and their significance.

After this, the dying person experiences a vision of redness as the red drop of life-energy inherited from his mother at conception wanders adrift from its home in the navel and begins to ascend the central channel. And a vision of whiteness floods the mind as the white drop inherited from the father at the time of conception falls from its home in the forehead and begins to descend through the central channel. As the dying person's breathing becomes longer and slower, there is the sense that the sun is setting, and then all becomes dark and unconscious. And then, when the red and white drops of the mother and father come together in the heart, one is suddenly awakened to bright joyful light and a feeling of blissful serenity. That is the special moment of the transitional phase between life and death. It is the moment of simple liberation. This is a wonderful moment.

Yet this radiant luminosity will appear to be very intense and frightening for those who have had no experience of it during their lifetimes. It is as if a photographic flash bulb were to blaze incandescently before our eyes. We instinctively blink and turn away in discomfort. For many people, the initial experience of the radiant luminosity of reality is the same. For them, it will be unbearably bright and yet will be gone in a fraction of a second. The Tibetan Book of the Dead talks of the various experiences that the deceased will encounter in terms of days. Sadly, these are not normally understood by Tibetan masters as normal human days. The length of time a person can remain in a meditative state with their minds calmly focussed and absorbed in non-duality is considered as a day here. So if you have not had any meditational experience beforehand, the entire period of forty-nine days, traditionally mentioned as the duration of the death phase until rebirth, may only last a matter of minutes. All the lights and visions will rush by in a blur with little chance of recognition. However, as the book says, we cannot say for certain how long any individual will remain in that transitional state between death and rebirth. So it is important to read the text over and over again — if nothing else, this act of kindness and devotion will generate great reserves of merit that can be dedicated to helping the deceased on their journey.

It is the Tibetan Buddhist view that all living beings, including animals, experience this radiant light just at the moment of true death. This experience occurs regardless of the particular faith or religious beliefs of the person involved. There is a certain amount of corroboration for this in the reports

of those in the West and elsewhere who have returned from near-death experiences. However, one should be cautious in equating the two experiences since, from a Buddhist point of view, such individuals have not truly died. Perhaps they are just experiencing the phenomena described earlier that precede actual death. Death itself is said to have occurred only when blood and lymph begin to trickle from the nostrils of the corpse.

A SEQUENCE OF VISIONS

Failure to recognize this radiant luminosity for the moment of easy liberation that it is will result in the dying person experiencing a sequence of visions of various spiritual beings. All people will see these, however fleetingly, except advanced yogins who were able to liberate themselves at the time of the radiant luminosity. It is also said that extremely evil people do not experience these visions, for immediately after their death they hurtle down to the hell realms! Since this book is Buddhist in origin, the various beings who appear are described in terms of well-known Buddhas and their attendants. They are often termed "deities" but this should not be understood in a conventional sense. For they are not really gods at all, but embodiments in Tibetan cultural guise of the various facets of enlightenment that inhere within our own primordial minds. In this sense they are projections, whether they appear in peaceful loving forms or wrathful terrifying shapes. Just as we project our beliefs and paranoias upon the world and its inhabitants around us during our lifetimes, so also when we are dead do the true qualities of our primordial mind appear in whatever forms we clothe them in. Tibetan lamas working with Westerners of different religious backgrounds generally state that these visions will take on the appearances of whatever religious imagery we are familiar with. Hence, a Christian will perhaps see a similar range of beings but in the form of Jesus and his saints, or later as demons and devils. Anybody using this book who is not a Buddhist following the Tibetan tradition should bear this in mind and possibly make changes necessary to feel comfortable with the imagery. The task remains the same: recognize them as manifestations of your own spiritual energies and qualities, then you will gain liberation and beatitude.

THE SIX MODES OF EXISTENCE

If a person experiences these visions but fails to recognize them for what they are, then they will inevitably begin the process that results in rebirth. This is linked with the concept of reincarnation, found in many other religions apart from Buddhism. The book gives a whole range of instructions by which the dead person can try to avoid this outcome. Even if they have to be reborn, the book gives help to avoid rebirth in any of the modes of existence that are not conducive to spiritual growth. There are traditionally six modes of existence described in Buddhist scriptures. It is said that a predominance of any one particular type of negativity results in rebirth in the most appropriate mode. Thus, pride leads to rebirth as a god, jealousy as a demi-god, attachment as a human being, stupidity as an animal, greed as a hungry ghost and hatred as a hell denizen. If we choose, we do not have to understand these modes of existence solely in literal terms. Figuratively speaking, these modes can be seen as psychological states,

given the Buddhist idea that all things are shaped and formed by the mind. For example, a god would be a person who lives a life of luxury and ease, perhaps like a rich Californian, and so forth. Yet literal or figurative, only the human state, the mode that is balanced without too much suffering and too much comfort, is said to be conducive to future spiritual growth. An excess of suffering prevents people from ever giving thought to anything else since their minds are overwhelmed by pain, while an excess of comfort and happiness dulls the mind and gives no motivation for change. If all else fails, the deceased person is instructed to seek rebirth as a human.

HOW TO USE THE TEACHINGS

❊

The Tibetan Book of the Dead *is primarily concerned with methods that enable people to pass skill-fully through the process of death without succumbing to the many dangers that will be encountered. If used to guide a dying person, the best results will be obtained if that person was previously familiar with the contents of the book. Traditionally, people wishing to use these teachings during their lifetime would receive the appropriate ceremony of initiation which authorizes them to employ the meditation techniques outlined by the text. This level of practice is related to advanced tantric practices involving intensive meditation and visualization which require years of preparatory training. It is considered inappropriate and dangerous to attempt such practices without the personal guidance of a qualified master. However, there are some practices that the interested beginner could usefully undertake. A review of one's lifestyle and a determined attempt to avoid grossly immoral deeds and thoughts is viewed as the most important foundation for a spiritual life. If the person finds it congenial, they should also try to develop a sense of devotion through prayer and the recitation of mantras. When a degree of moral and emotional stability has been achieved, they can apply themselves to the most basic form of Buddhist meditation.*

BEGINNING TO MEDITATE

❋

When beginning to meditate, the learner should set aside a particular time of the day and initially allow themselves about thirty minutes for the practice. As mentioned in the commentary to the text, a quiet and pleasant room with some religious symbols is very helpful. Learners should sit comfortably with upright backs either in the traditional cross-legged position or else on a firm chair. The eyes should be half-closed, looking downward about four feet ahead. The learners should then focus on the movement of their breath as it enters and leaves their nostrils. It is helpful to count each breath, one for breathing out and then two for breathing in, and so on up until ten. They should then restart and continue in this way for the duration of the meditation period. At first it will be found that the mind is easily distracted and wanders off along chains of irrelevant thoughts. When the beginner notices that this has happened, there is no reason for anger or frustration. This state of distraction is quite natural. All that needs to be done is to note that this has happened and then return to watching and counting the breaths. Anyone who applies

themselves to this regularly and carefully will soon notice some changes in their daily life. The mind will become clearer and calmer and less disturbed by negative thoughts and emotions. When a degree of skill has been achieved, one can move on to other forms of meditation such as that which develops insight. However, more advanced meditation cannot simply be taught from a book as the techniques and themes should be tailored to the aptitude and personality of the individual. It is hoped that the beginner will by this stage have contacted somebody who is able to give them the expert guidance that they need.

THE HISTORY OF THE TEXTS

This book is an abridged and simplified version of that work popularly known in the West as the Tibetan Book of the Dead. Though there may be some who will frown upon this attempt to render the text more accessible to the general reader in the West with little familiarity with Buddhism, the original text includes much material that presupposes a lifetime of training and deep understanding of Buddhism. It is hoped therefore that this version will be of some use for those in extremis who have not had the good fortune to encounter Buddhist teachings in depth during their lifetimes. The reader may however be assured that, even in its simplified form, nothing of intrinsic value has been omitted in this book. Instead, the key elements of the instructions are presented as they are in the original Tibetan text, but without the distracting doctrinal discussions and complicated advanced teachings, so that the book will be beneficial to a greater range of people, whether Buddhist or not. Those who are already familiar with Tibetan Buddhist teachings and practice must decide for themselves whether to use this book or one of the complete versions that are available in translation.

Actually, there is no work with such a name in the Tibetan tradition. Rather, there exists a huge corpus of teachings and scriptures dealing with the particular problems faced by the dying and the dead. This particular work, called the Great Liberation through Hearing in the Transitional Phase, comes from a large collection of several hundred texts, known as the Cycle of the Peaceful and Wrathful Deities. These are said to have been taught by a great Indian mystic, Padmasambhava, who was one of the first teachers of Buddhism to visit Tibet during the eighth century CE. Foreseeing times of persecution and chaos, these among other texts were buried as religious treasures in various locations around Tibet. When peace had returned and the times were auspicious, later mystics endowed with special clairvoyant powers were able to locate these texts and bring them forth for the welfare of beings.

Our book was rediscovered by Karma Lingpa in the fourteenth century in a cave in the Gampo hills of central Tibet. Though the collection he discovered includes many aspects of Buddhist practices, the text presented here merely covers the experiences to be encountered in the three transitional phases of dying, death and rebirth. There are similar works in this collection, which deal with three other transitional phases: life itself, dreaming and meditation. One hopes that these also will eventually be translated, but in the meanwhile we have this Great Liberation through the Transitional Phases of Dying, Death, and Rebirth. It is Tibet's gift to humanity — let us treasure it and put it to good use!

Stephen Hodge

THE GREAT LIBERATION THROUGH HEARING IN THE TRANSITIONAL PHASE OF DEATH

THIS GREAT *Liberation through Hearing* is the technique by which average people following a spiritual discipline may be liberated while in the transitional phases of dying and death. Though people today are more accustomed to acquiring knowledge through the written word, most Eastern cultures, including that of Tibet, lay great stress on the oral transmission of wisdom. The importance we attach to the written word can even be seen in the popular, though inaccurate, title this text is given in the West — the Tibetan Book of the Dead. In contrast, the Tibetans themselves know it as the Great Liberation through Hearing. Of course, when this text is used by a guide to assist the dying and the dead, he or she will inevitably need to read it aloud. However, instruction through the spoken word is normal in everyday circumstances because it is believed to be a better method of ensuring understanding and spiritual growth, for unlike the written word, oral teachings can be tailored to the needs of the recipient.

THE OPENING PHASE

S O OFTEN, people do not care to think of their own deaths seriously while they are healthy and it is often too late when sickness and old age beset them. Yet to prepare for death when one has the opportunity is not a morbid undertaking, but a mark of spiritual maturity and wisdom. The teachings in this book can be used as the basis for meditation during one's lifetime and many of its insights will help foster an understanding of the psychological and emotional forces at work during life. The more familiar a person becomes with these processes, the better able will he or she be to make sense of the events which are said to be experienced during and after death.

The person who intends to use this book in an attempt to help guide the spirit of somebody on his or her deathbed should also be familiar with the contents. He or she should practice reading it aloud smoothly and clearly, while reflecting on the meaning. In this way, the would-be guide will be better able to help the dying person through familiarity with the instructions in the text. When reciting the passages, the guide should remember at all times that he or she is acting for the dying or dead person. If the guide has problems with the phenomenon of death, it is better to deal with them first. All negativity or ego-inspired thoughts on the part of the guide will act as impediments in the task being attempted. A guide should be fearless and confident in order to inspire the dying person.

THE PRELIMINARY INSTRUCTIONS

※

YOU SHOULD VIGOROUSLY apply yourself to this *Great Liberation through Hearing* while passing through the transitional phase of death. Somebody, such as a trusted fellow practitioner or else a close friend, should act as a guide and read this *Liberation through Hearing* with a calm and clear voice by the head of the deceased person. If there is no body, the person reading the text should sit on the bed or a chair that belonged to the deceased person. He should speak with sincerity and draw the spirit of the deceased to him.

Visualizing the deceased to be present before him, the guide should then read this text. While doing this, the family and close friends of the deceased person should be asked to be silent as the sounds of their weeping and sobbing will be very disturbing to the spirit of the deceased. If there is a body, then the guide should read this *Great Liberation through Hearing* three or seven times in a whisper close to the ears of the deceased, during the period of time that occurs after the gross outer breathing has ceased but not the inner subtle breath.

commentary

The *Great Liberation through Hearing* is primarily a guidebook to assist those who are passing through the confusing experiences of death and rebirth. Yet at the same time, many of its instructions have an implicit relevance for those who are still coping with the challenges of everyday life. We can draw the most valuable lessons from this book if we are presently engaged in ways of spiritual development, especially forms of meditational practice.

•

During our lifetimes we often need a spiritual friend who will help us when we have lost our way. If we have begun a process of regular meditation or prayer, the right type of environment is very beneficial. There should be nothing unpleasant in the room that may cause agitation because we should be able to focus our minds without disturbances and understand what we have been taught. It is all too easy for the untrained mind to go astray and fall victim to negative emotions and thoughts.

•

The dying person will find it most helpful to rest in a room arranged similarly to where we practice meditation and prayer. The text stresses the value of having a guide give these instructions to the dying person. If appropriate, we should light candles and incense and set out offerings such as dishes of tasty food. The atmosphere should be especially quiet and tranquil so that full attention is given to reading the text. If there is no corpse, it is helpful to have a portrait of the deceased in his or her place.

RECOGNIZING THE RADIANT LIGHT
THAT OCCURS DURING THE DYING PROCESS

❀

THE GUIDE SHOULD BEGIN by reading this for the person who is dying:

> *Listen, [Name]! You have now reached the moment*
> *when you should seek a path.*
> *Just as your breathing stops, you will begin*
> *to experience the primal radiant light*
> *that is the first phase of the death process,*
> *as shown to you by your teacher*
> *during your lifetime. It is reality itself,*
> *empty and unadorned like space.*
> *This is your primordial mind, unsullied*
> *and unadorned, devoid of center and boundaries,*
> *in its emptiness and radiance.*
> *When this happens, recognize this*
> *for what it is! Go into that state!*
> *When it happens,*
> *I shall help you recognize it.*

The guide should repeat this in the ear of the dying person over and over again until the gross outer breathing has stopped, so as to impress it upon him. When the dying person is just about to stop breathing, the guide should turn the person onto their right side, arranging their body into the sleeping lion's posture. The guide should also read the instructions at this time to help the dying person recognize what follows.

At this time, all beings experience the mind-energy associated with the structure of reality, free from any falsehood. This is the first phase of the dying process, called the radiant light of reality. Moreover, the period of time lasts from the cessation of the gross outer breath until the subtle inner breath also ceases. Ordinary people call this a state of unconsciousness. The duration of this period is not fixed, for this depends upon the relative goodness or evil of the person's life and the quality of their meditational practice. However, as most scriptures concerned with these teachings state that this period of unconsciousness lasts for four and a half days, the guide should attempt to help the deceased person recognize the nature of the radiant light for that number of days.

commentary

All Eastern religious traditions stress the importance of posture when engaged in meditation or prayer. Ideally, we should be seated with half-closed eyes, our legs crossed in the lotus position, and our back straight and head slightly inclined forward. Our breathing should be calm and natural, as this will influence the behavior of our minds.

When we encounter spiritual realities for the first time, whether just starting to meditate or at the time of death, our minds are usually inflexible with ingrained self-interest and belief in the reality of the everyday world. It is good to be as comfortable as possible for it is painful to witness the disintegration of our world as the senses upon which it was based crumble and dissolve.

•

The dying person should be helped to lie in the optimal position for death, the so-called "sleeping lion's posture." It is thought that this posture naturally calms the erratic flow of an agitated mind and thus it may be helpful to the dying person by allowing him to concentrate more easily.

A lifetime of habitual clinging to the outer objects of the senses while under the influence of desire and attachment, fear, loathing, disgust, and confusion, does not prepare people for spiritual growth let alone the reality of death . In such cases, the fading away of the senses and the loss of contact with their objects can be frightening. Left with no objects behind which to hide, the mind may be in a turmoil of anguish. With his or her emotions laid bare, the dying person may feel exposed and vulnerable. It is the role of spiritual friends and guides to soothe such fears and encourage the dying person with uplifting words of hope and good cheer.

IF THE DYING PERSON is able, he should apply the instructions himself that he received during his lifetime. If he is unable to do this, then a fellow practitioner or else a trusted friend should sit nearby the dying person. They should clearly read out the signs of death in sequence:

The mirage you are now experiencing is
the sign that the earth element is dissolving into
the water element.
Now the smoke is the sign that the water element is
dissolving into the fire element.
Now the glowing fireflies are the sign
that the fire element is dissolving
into the wind element.
Now the flickering candle-flame is the sign that
the wind element is dissolving
into consciousness.
Now this white moonlit sky is the sign
that consciousness is dissolving
into "appearance."
Now this red sunlit sky is the sign that "appearance"
is dissolving into "increase."
Now this dark night sky is the sign that "increase"
is dissolving into "attainment."
Now this twilight sky is the sign of "attainment"
dissolving into the radiant light.

commentary

The so-called "signs of death" are very similar to those experienced by expert meditators as they progress beyond the confines of the everyday world. Unlike accomplished meditators, ordinary people tend to find these experiences unpleasant, and their outer world, that was once so solid, becomes like a dream in the morning sun.

As the sense of vision fades, the eyes cannot be opened or closed and the body grows weak, tired, and heavy. The complexion grows dull and the dying person experiences a hazy, bluish mirage shimmering uncertainly in their sight. As the sense of hearing fades, the monotonous sound of background murmuring ceases, and the ears hear nothing any more. The body fluids dry up and the dying person experiences a vision of puffs of smoke rising to the sky. As the sense of smell fades, the breath becomes unbalanced so that inhalation is weak and exhalation strong. Odors of any kind can no longer be detected and the dying person experiences a vision of sparks before their eyes. As the

sense of taste dies away, the tongue grows thick and fills the mouth. It turns blue at the root and diminishes in length. All breathing ceases and neither taste nor physical sensations can be detected. Internally, the dying person has a vision of a short burst of light, like the final flaming of a candle upon the point of extinction.

People are said to have a kind of spiritual physiology that comprises a structure of energy pathways or channels and the subtle energies that flow through them. As consciousness itself begins to weaken, the subtle energies abiding in the upper parts of the right and left channels merge at the crown of the head. They enter the central channel and dislodge a white bead-like drop of energy that was received from the father at the time of conception. This falls downward and a vision of whiteness is experienced. It is called "appearance" because it appears like bright moonlight, and it is also called "empty" because consciousness is now very weak.

As the subtle energies that dwell in the lower parts of the right and left channels merge at the base of the torso and enter the central channel, a red bead-like drop of energy that was received from the mother at the time of conception is pushed slowly upward. A red light appears which is called "increase of appearance" because it is brighter than before. It is also known as "very empty" because the conscious mind is now very weak.

As the upper energies move downward and the lower energies rise up, the white and red beads of energy meet at the heart and there is an experience of total blackness. This is not like an external darkness, but is bright and glowing. It is called "near attainment" because it is close to the end, and it is also called "great empty" because it is utterly devoid of any other characteristics. When all internal processes have come to an end, all that remains of the subtle mind dissolves into the radiant light. This can be experienced either at death or through meditation.

WHEN THIS PROCESS is nearing completion, the guide should encourage the dying person to fix his mind upon the following aspiration:

*N*ow *that the process of so-called dying is upon*
    you, frame your mind thus:
"Though the time of dying has descended upon me,
    I should rely upon this process
    of dying and generate a spirit imbued solely
    with the aspiration for enlightenment,
    that is, love and compassion.
    I must achieve perfect buddhahood
    for the sake of all beings who are as extensive in
    number as space."
You should generate this attitude, but in particular
    you should also think this:
"I must recognize the radiant light of dying
    as the embodiment of reality and within that state
    achieve the supreme accomplishment,

the spiritual structure of being.
I shall then act for the benefit of all beings.
    Though I may not achieve this,
    I shall at least recognize the dying phase
    for what it is and make manifest the embodiment of
    the spiritual structure of being that is conjoined
    with the dying phase. I shall then work for the
    benefit of all beings, who are as extensive in
    number as boundless space, appearing in whatever
    form is needed to train any being."
Without letting this fervent wish slip from your mind,
    you should now recollect the application of the
    instructions previously given that are familiar
    to you.

The guide should instruct the dying person quietly and clearly, speaking close to his ear, reminding him ceaselessly how to experience this.

commentary

When the Buddha began his ministry in India, the first thing that he taught was the truth of suffering – that our lives are dominated by frustration, dissatisfaction, and misery. Even when we feel that we are experiencing joy, the few fleeting joys we encounter while trapped in the prison of negative emotions are worthless compared to the bliss of true awakening. It is difficult, however, to break out of that prison while the objects of desire and aversion are at hand, taunting us with their seeming reality.

The easiest time to practice the path of renunciation is at the point of death. Then the illusion of solid reality has melted away, and the habitual memory patterns of the dying person have not yet arisen to confuse him or her with their dreamlike specters of a solid world in which they can immerse themselves and lose their way once more. This point, when the subtle mind encounters radiant light, is a moment of greatest opportunity. All connection with the previous life has been completely cut off and the mind of the dying person is, for a brief while only, naked and free.

AFTER RESPIRATION has ceased, the guide should instruct him as follows:

Listen, [Name]! The pure radiance of reality has dawned and is now present for you. Recognize it!

This present aspect of your awareness that is pure and unformed, this very unformed purity devoid of any substance, attributes or colors, is reality, the All-good Mother.

Yet this unformed awareness of yours is not just a blank emptiness, for your awareness is also free from all limitations; it is sparkling, radiant, and vibrant. This is the primordial mind, enlightenment, the All-good Father.

These two aspects of your awareness: unformed emptiness and radiant vibrancy are indivisible in their presence. They form the embodiment of reality as enlightenment.

This indivisible radiance and emptiness of your awareness is present as a mass of luminosity. Herein there is no birth or death, for this is the awakened state of unchanging light. To know just this is enough.

Knowing this pure aspect of your awareness is to know yourself as an enlightened being; for you thus to behold your own awareness is to establish yourself in the realized mind state of enlightenment.

The guide should repeat this correctly and clearly three or seven times. In this way, it is certain that the dying person will remember what he has been taught in the past, recognize this radiant luminosity as his bare awareness, and then become inseparably merged with the embodiment of reality and be liberated.

commentary

Very positive benefits will be felt in our spiritual lives if we try to purify our minds by sincere and repentant confession of all our past misdeeds and negative patterns of thought. When we go to sleep or undergo the experience of death, we should feel that we are welcomed into the loving embrace of our primordial All-good parents. From the beginning of endless time, we have been supported and nourished by our All-good Mother of endless space. It is she who provided the opportunity for our coming into being, for our growth and well-being. It is she who accommodates our desires and tolerates our anger. From the beginning of endless time it is our primordial All-good Father, the impulse to exist, that has urged us on to create a world of our own volition. Whatever mistakes have been made are naturally forgiven if arrogance and conceit are abandoned and we face our true condition with naked humility and uplifted heart. Let us return like children to our true parents and be reunited in joy!

During our lifetimes, we should try to minimize our attachment to concerns of this life. When faced with death, it is too late to worry about unfinished work, and whatever remains to be done must be attended to by others. The dying person must leave the company of relatives and friends and go off alone. In the solitude of his or her own luminous mind, it is important that the dying person suffers no attachment to what has been experienced before.

37

THE DYING PERSON will be liberated if they recognize this first radiant luminosity, but if he is afraid and does not recognize it, a second radiant luminosity will appear about half an hour after his breathing has stopped. Then the deceased person's consciousness will slip out of his body, though he will not realize what has happened, uncertain whether he has died or not. He will see his loved ones as before and go to them. He will even hear them weeping.

At this stage, the guide should instruct the deceased person again before the intense delusory experiences that arise through karma occur and terrifying horrors of death descend upon him.

At this point, the deceased person should be reminded of the meditational practices he cultivated when he was alive. If he did not do anything in particular, he should be instructed to visualize compassion embodied as any spiritual being that is appropriate. The circumstances of the deceased person's life and death may also make it difficult for him to remember what he was previously taught, so guidance during this phase is very important.

commentary

Spiritual practice during our lifetime is of supreme importance. If we are given authentic instructions and training, we should, in time, become familiar with the kind of experiences that we will encounter at the time of death. This will enable us to recognize the otherwise disorientating visions that arise after death for what they are in reality.

•

Remembering the teachings on the frustrating condition of endless rebirth, the deceased person must attempt to abandon all that binds him or her to the world and resolve to escape from the cycle of existence. They may thus attain the bliss of liberation for themselves. But to remain content with their own salvation is not enough. At the time of death, people hear the weeping of those who mourn their passing, Yet they should not be attached to their loved ones for they have their own destinies. Instead, the deceased should be filled with compassion for the sorrow of the mourners, and they should now make a resolution to strive toward the attainment of buddhahood for the sake of those they have left behind. Even if we are not dying, we should regularly frame our minds in this way at the beginning of any session of meditation.

•

In all the great religions of the world, compassion and love are thought to form part of the supreme being, be it God, Allah or the Buddha. This compassion is often seen to manifest in particular forms, and so it is helpful for us to bring to mind whatever image of compassion and love we find most congenial. This will help to calm and reassure us as well as providing us with inspiration for our own spiritual growth. When experiencing death or just facing life's difficulties, a sincere belief and trust in the power and kindness of such a being will be beneficial, and increase the chances of emerging safely from those experiences.

IT IS BEST if the deceased person comes to understand what he is experiencing during the first phase of the dying process, but if he has not done so then the guide should remind him during the second phase. His awareness will be awakened by this and then he will be liberated. Whereas before his consciousness did not grasp whether he was dead or not, it now becomes lucid during this phase. This is called the pure astral body. If the deceased person understands the instructions at this point, his individual reality will encounter the matrix reality and he will be freed from the bonds of karma. Just as darkness is dispelled by the light of the sun, so also will the power of karma be dispelled by the radiant luminosity of the path and he will be liberated. This second phase of the dying process is vividly experienced by the astral body of the deceased, and his consciousness will once again be able to hear what is said. If the deceased person can understand the instructions at this point, their aim will be achieved. Since the delusive experiences generated by his karma have not yet arisen, he is still able to transform himself in any way. So, even if the deceased person has not recognized the primal radiant luminosity, he can still be liberated by recognizing the luminosity of the second phase of the dying process.

commentary

If we have not bothered with our spiritual development, from time to time we will encounter particularly unpleasant experiences during our lives. Yet such experiences have their roots within our own attitudes and behavior. If we continually indulge in negative deeds and have allowed our minds to become dominated by aggression, greed, and stupidity, we are likely to encounter projections of this unwholesomeness. We may feel that the whole world is a hostile place and its inhabitants are our enemies trying to destroy us. Through meditation it is possible for us to analyze such unpleasant experiences, and identify the negative patterns of thought and behavior which give rise to them. By identifying the underlying causes, we can then work on our inner selves and gradually rid ourselves of such negative traits.

•

At the time of death, those who have led thoroughly evil lives will have a vision of the terrifying Lord of Death and his henchmen in whatever form they have been culturally conditioned to expect. The guide must try hard at this time to reassure those who are frightened that these terrible apparitions are merely projections of his or her own mind. He should remind the dying person to have faith in the goodness that surrounds him or her and not to be afraid.

If the deceased person has led a wholesome life of virtue, they will see themselves surrounded by hosts of divine beings who will call out to him or her by name and invite him or her to accompany them to paradise. Abandoning all attachment to their present body, they should relax their minds and then gather together all that remains of his or her consciousness and follow these heavenly messengers upward and out of the body to a pure realm of awareness and bliss.

Advanced meditators often choose to meet death face to face, sitting upright in the posture of profound contemplation. It is said that the consciousness of such people departs from their bodies at this time in a blaze of rainbow light from the crown of the head and flies off into the realm of the sky. Such people have no need of instruction or guidance at the time of their death. Ordinary people with little or no experience of meditation, however, may be frightened and much in need of help. The guide should remember this and act with compassion.

THE VISIONS OF THE REALITY PHASE

NOW THE DECEASED PERSON *begins their journey through a series of strange visions. Whether he or she is able to make sense of what he or she experiences will depend upon his or her previous preparation, and also the skill of the guide. As mentioned previously, the precise details and forms of these visions are probably determined by culture and religion, and hence will differ for each individual. It is likely that the sequence of specific colors at each stage will remain constant for all people. Tibetans believe that the forms of the visions described here are what they will experience after death. The imagery derives from the meditational experiences of masters of great spiritual accomplishment — in the view of this collection of teachings, both meditation and dreams are also intermediate or transitional phases whose structure can often parallel that of the death phase.*

To help those without the ability to encounter these visions spontaneously during their lifetime, the various beings which appear in the text are often depicted together in a mandalalike arrangement to assist recognition. The beings tend to be grouped together according to the days when they will appear to the deceased. Basically, they form three groups: the peaceful beings, the stern beings, and the wrathful ones. The kindly peaceful beings are said to emanate from one's heart region and are linked to the physical body; the stern ones arise from one's throat and hence are linked to speech; and the wrathful beings emerge within one's head which is the seat of thought.

42

THE PEACEFUL VISIONS

IF THE DECEASED PERSON has not been liberated even by that, then the next stage, the reality transitional phase, will be experienced, during which delusive experiences generated by karma will occur. Hence, it is vital to read these powerful and helpful instructions to show him the nature of the reality phase.

By now his loved ones will be weeping and moaning, his meals will no longer be served, his clothes will be packed away and his bed stripped.

The deceased person will see his relatives, but they will be unable to see him. He will hear them calling out to him but they will not hear him answering them. Filled with grief, he will drift away. During this phase, experiences of luminosity, noise and dazzling colors will occur that may cause the deceased person to feel faint with fear, terror and anxiety. At this time, the guide should give this great introduction to the reality transitional phase.

commentary

As we go through life, the experiences we encounter depend largely upon our own minds. Tibetan Buddhism teaches that the mind does not passively receive images of the world but actually creates and projects them onto the sense impressions of bare reality, using its store of memories and habitual traits. For this reason, few of us ever experience reality as it is in actuality, but instead overlay it with a host of our own projections. These projections are usually negative in nature.

According to our level of inner growth, we may be able to modify these self-created visions into forms and images that are more conducive to our spiritual health and growth. Their hallucinatory nature becomes more apparent at the time of death as well as when we become more accomplished in meditation.

If only we can let go of our needs and fears, then we can come to terms with such projections. If we can let go, we will come to rest in the natural state of the mind. For this profound experience to occur, our confused minds must be soothed and all our fears pacified by the compassion and skill of our spiritual friends and guides.

•

During the death process, people encounter bright lights, tumultuous noise, and a bewildering array of scintillating colors that overawe them. They have left the physical realm behind, and now, free of all impurity, these visions spontaneously manifest themselves as though in unrestricted play. It is important that the deceased person should not try to interrupt the flow of colors, lights, and forms, for these are the natural expressions of spiritual energies. At this time, it is vital for the deceased person to understand that he or she is now dead. Any idea of connection with, or separation from, friends and relatives must be abandoned as futile illusion.

THE GUIDE SHOULD CALL the deceased person by his name and instruct them in a clear and precise voice:

Listen carefully, [Name]! You did not recognize the radiant luminosity that occurred yesterday as you were dying so you have now drifted into this phase of reality. Recognize what I describe to you without becoming distracted!

You are now experiencing what people call 'death'. You are now drifting away from this world, but you are not unique, for this happens to everybody. Though you feel longing and attachment to this life, you cannot stay here but must wander lost through cyclical existence. Give up longing and attachment and bring to mind whatever symbols of spiritual ideals that are familiar to you!

No matter what terrifying experiences arise during the reality phase, do not forget these words! Remember their meaning as you go forth.

The essential point is to recognize your experiences through them.

"Now that I am experiencing the reality phase, I must abandon all hateful and terrifying hallucinations.

Let me recognize whatever appears as the natural manifestation of my own mind, knowing that this is how this phase is experienced.

Now that I have come to this vital juncture, let me not fear the peaceful and wrathful beings, for these are only projections arising from my own mind."

Recite these words clearly, remembering their meaning as you go forth. Do not forget them, for they are a key to recognizing all the terrifying experiences you may encounter as your own projections.

commentary

We should consider ourselves most fortunate if we have encountered these teachings concerning the superficial and the profound aspects of reality. From time without beginning, each of us has wandered around the cycle of existence in total bewilderment and ignorance. Again and again, we have taken birth in various states of misery, and all of us have continuously responded to our situation with a confused jumble of emotions. Endlessly tossed about upon this turbulent sea of emotion, we are sometimes happy and sometimes sad. Weeping or laughing, from moment to moment we feel frightened, angry, alone, and vulnerable, or suddenly full of pride and arrogance, cheered up by some trifle and full of confidence. Puffed up with self-importance, we are now ready to criticize and condemn the rest of the world for not being as good as us.

Whirling around and around, these feelings are all centered upon our notion of self. Yet Buddhism teaches that our so-called self, the ego, is a parasitical illusion without any substantial existence, something that has been constructed as a defense mechanism to deal with the experience of impermanence. It is this illusory self that suffers the full onslaught of our emotional turmoil. As it strives to create itself out of empty space and become solid, the ego-self always feels paranoid that it will be discovered for what it is – a hollow illusion. It works hard to maintain its status of "self importance" and suffers greatly as the all-encompassing reality of great space continuously dissolves the fabric of its being. Having no basis in reality, the ego-self keeps crumbling away and must be constantly reinvented. It reacts with delight when it meets with a situation that seems to protect it from damage.

When your mind parts from your body, the visions of pure reality will shine forth, shimmering like a summer mirage on the plains. They are subtle yet clear; distinctly experienced, they will fill you with fear and anxiety. Do not be fearful or afraid of them! Do not be anxious! They are the glowing radiance of your reality so recognize them as such!

A great roar of noise will reverberate forth from within the light, like the sound of a thousand crashes of thunder rumbling at the same time. This is the natural sound of your reality so do not be fearful or afraid of it! Do not be anxious! You now have an astral body generated by the energy of your habitual tendencies, not a physical one of flesh and blood. No matter what sounds, dazzling colors, or radiant luminosity occur, they cannot hurt you or cause your death. Just recognize them as your own projections and all will be well. Know that this is the reality phase of death!

No matter what religious practices you did during your life, if you have not received these instructions and do not recognize these experiences to be your own projections, then you will be terrified by the luminosity, alarmed by the sounds and frightened by the dazzling colors. If you don't comprehend the essential point of this instruction, you will wander lost in cyclical existence, not having understood the luminosity, the sounds, and dazzling colors for what they are.

commentary

If we constantly apply ourselves to meditation practice during the course of our lives, we may be able, though with some difficulty, to strip away all the supports that maintain the illusion of the ego-self. However, the material fabric of the ego's support – both the world and the physical body – is destroyed by death and all contact with its "friends" is severed. Now the mind is truly left to its own devices and its experience of reality is much more direct and immediate. The worldly concerns which formerly served as the support of the ego have all been stripped away and the insubstantial nature of its condition has been exposed in all its falsity. It was never really real at all, and the awesome power of this truth may strike the consciousness like a bombshell!

Bewildered by the dazzling display of lights, the deceased may fail to recognize them as manifestations of his or her own spiritual energy. Overwhelmed by their intensity, he or she may not be able to make any sense of them. In fact, they are the projections arising from his or her own chaotic mind. The guide, therefore, should offer the deceased person counsel and assistance to enable him or her to recognize these visions for what they are.

These spiraling rainbows of light take on the shapes of various divine beings, initially in peaceful groups but later in terrifying images of wrath. These become embodiments of the deceased's spiritual energies, and array themselves in mandalalike patterns that reveal the spiritual structure of the universe and form the great mandala of primordial enlightenment. They are like the facets of a diamond, each unique in itself yet all belonging to the whole.

THE PEACEFUL VISIONS OF THE FIRST DAY

Having been unconscious for four and a half days, you will now move on. When you wake up again, you will wonder what has happened to you. Recognize this state as the reality phase of death. During this time, ordinary cyclical existence is suspended and all experience will occur in the form of luminosity and images.

All of space will shine with deep sky-blue light. The white Blessed Vairochana come from the central buddha-realm, Ghanavyuha, and appear to you. He is seated upon a lion-throne, holding an eight-spoked wheel in his hands and embracing his consort, the Lady of the Space Realm. The blue luminosity of consciousness in its natural purity, the intensely dazzling radiant and clear azure-blue of the awareness of the continuum of reality, will shine out and pervade you from the heart of the Blessed Vairochana and his consort. This light is so brilliant that you can hardly bear to look at it.

At the same time, the soft white light associated with the gods will also shine forth and penetrate you. Because of your negative karmic deeds, you will then be afraid of the azure-blue light and try to flee in terror from this awareness of the continuum of reality. Instead, you will feel attracted and drawn to the soft white light of the gods.

commentary

Both during meditation and after death, dramatic changes occur to the normal structure of the mind. The habit patterns of defiled ignorance are absorbed into the spacious great expanse of fundamental reality, and just for a moment there arises a precious opportunity of relaxing the mind in its entirety. This phase does not last long. While we always have the chance to repeat this experience during our lifetimes, this is not the case for the dead. The guide should urgently impress the special value of this fleeting moment upon the deceased person. Here, in the short transitional space between one lifetime of confusion and the next, the radiant blue light of one's intrinsic primary awareness briefly dawns. The dead person must not allow him- or herself to be overwhelmed by this blinding light. They should not be shocked by its purity for, in reality, the multiplicity of worldly objects is an illusion. This stark simplicity is the true, open ground from which all the prolific complexity of habitual experience arises.

The core facet of the intrinsic enlightened mind also manifests as Vairochana, the Illuminator. He is accompanied by his consort, the Lady of the Space Realm. As with all the other beings who will appear, they are joined in sexual union to symbolize the interdependence of the particular aspect of enlightenment that they represent.

Do not be frightened of the intensely bright clear
azure-blue light of the supreme awareness.
It is the radiant light of this enlightened being,
the awareness of the continuum of reality.
Try to feel drawn to it with trust and devotion,
and pray thus: 'This is the radiant light of the
Blessed Vairochana's compassion: I will go to it for
refuge!'. It is the Blessed Vairochana coming to
lead you from the dangers of this phase of death.
It is the radiant light of his compassion.
Do not be attracted to the soft white light of the gods,
do not be attached to it or drawn to it! If you are
drawn to it, you will wander lost into the realm of
the gods and continue to be reborn and die among
the six states of cyclical existence. Do not even
look at it, for it is a blockage to the path to
liberation. Instead, put your trust in the dazzling
azure-blue light, with intense devotion to the
Blessed Vairochana and his consort,
repeating this prayer with me:
"When I wander through the cycle of existence
driven by powerful ignorance,
may the Blessed Vairochana go before me
on the luminous path of radiant reality awareness,
with his consort, the Lady of the Space Realm,
behind me.
May they save me from fearful dangers in
the death phase and escort me to the
state of perfect enlightenment!"

By uttering this prayer with ardent trust and devotion, the deceased person will dissolve as rainbow light into the heart of Vairochana and his consort and become a transfigured celestial buddha in the central buddha-realm of Ghanavyuha.

commentary

Our minds have two aspects: that which is primordially enlightened and replete with all spiritual qualities and that which is a corrupted version of enlightenment. Vairochana and his consort are the embodiment of our intrinsic awareness and, at the same time, they also represent ultimate reality. Each of the Buddhas who appear on successive days represents other aspects of the enlightened mind. If the dead person is burdened with negative emotions and thoughts, they will be unable to recognize these aspects. Instead, their energy becomes distorted and solidifies as everyday reality. Each time the dead person fails to recognize them, they are gradually recreating the world they have left behind with all its sufferings. At the same time as the brilliant azure-blue associated with the person's intrinsic awareness appears, there is a less intense but seductive white light. In this context this symbolizes the world of the gods which is generated by negative pride and arrogance. The dead person's previous tendencies may make them feel more comfortable with this light and they are in danger of drifting away. Yet if they can let go of pride and ignorance they will cease to fear the radiance of reality and effortlessly merge with it. This embodiment of their intrinsic awareness is not passive: it radiates compassion and tries to draw the dead person to it. If they have the courage and strength to surrender to this vision of compassion, they will be absorbed into Vairochana's heart and thereby return to the very core of their own true being.

THE PEACEFUL VISIONS OF THE SECOND DAY

HOWEVER, IT IS POSSIBLE that the deceased person will be frightened by the luminosity and shafts of light and flee them because of habitual anger and negative deeds, even though the guide has given him these instructions. He is still confused even though he has recited the previous prayer, so on the second day he will encounter the Blessed Akshobhya and his entourage as well as his own negative karma which will lead him to the hell realm. Once again the guide should instruct the deceased person, calling him by name:

Listen carefully, [Name]! On this second day, the white luminosity of the pure water element will shine forth. At this point, the Blessed Akshobhya will come from the blue eastern realm of Abhirati and appear before you. He is blue in color and holds a vajra in his hand. Seated upon an elephant throne, he embraces his consort, Buddha-lochana. He is accompanied by two male bodhisattvas, Kshitigarbha and Maitreya, and two goddesses, Lasya and Pushpa.

The white luminosity of form in its natural purity, the intensely dazzling radiant and clear white of the mirror-like awareness, will shine out and pervade you from the heart of the Blessed Akshobhya and his consort. This light is so brilliant that you can hardly bear to look at it.

At the same time, the soft smoky light associated with the hell realm will also shine forth and penetrate you. Because of your habitual anger and hatred, you will then be afraid of the white light and try to flee in terror from it. Instead, you will feel attracted and drawn to the soft smoky light of the hell realm.

commentary

If the dead person has been weakened by countless lifetimes of erroneous notions and ignorance, they may not have the ability to endure a glimpse of their own mind's essential radiance and it will vanish as they try to hide from it. Feeling threatened by the vastness of its open nature, they may become hostile and self-protective. Unable to withstand the experience of limitless expansion, they may react by curling in upon themselves, and mentally turning away from all that spaciousness in order to shut themselves off from the all-encompassing terror.

At this point that aspect of the dying person's consciousness arises which is the subtle awareness that sees forms, but without clinging to them as though they were truly real. It is as if the mind were a perfectly clear mirror in which all that it encounters is reflected without bias or distortion. Everything is sharp and precise, perfectly focussed and appropriate in its own place. Nothing is added or omitted and no single aspect of the total picture is given any priority over another. Relaxed and aware, this "mirrorlike" consciousness sees everything simply in terms of color and form, and makes no attempt to read any-thing more into the situation than that. Entirely free of judgment, this awareness sees the complex web of cause and effect and remains quietly detached, uninvolved, and unconcerned.

Do not be frightened of the intensely bright clear
white light, but recognize it as the radiant light of
awareness. Try to feel drawn to it with trust and
devotion, and pray thus: "This is the radiant light
of the Blessed Akshobhya's compassion: I will go
to it for refuge!". It is the Blessed Akshobhya
coming to lead you from the terrors of this phase
of death. It is the hooklike radiant light of
Akshobhya's compassion, so put your trust in it!

Do not be attracted to the soft smoky light of the hell
realm! It is the enticing path formed by negative
deeds accumulated through your intense hatred and
anger. If you are drawn to it, you will fall into the
hell realm and be sucked into the muddy swamp of
unbearable misery with no hope of escape.

Do not even look at it, for it is a blockage to the
path to liberation. Abandon all your hatred and
anger! Instead, put your trust in the dazzling
white radiant light, with intense devotion to the
Blessed Akshobhya and his consort, repeating
this prayer with me:

"When I wander through the cycle of existence
    driven by intense anger and hatred,
    may the Blessed Akshobhya go before me
    on the luminous path of mirror-like awareness,
    with his consort, Buddha-lochana, behind me.

May they save me from fearful dangers in the
    death phase and escort me to the state of
    perfect enlightenment!"

By uttering this prayer with ardent trust and
devotion, the deceased person will dissolve as
rainbow light into the heart of Akshobhya and
become a transfigured celestial buddha in the
eastern buddha-realm of Abhirati.

commentary

As another facet of enlightenment, this awareness manifests itself in the image of Akshobhya, the Imperturbable, in union with his consort Buddha-lochana, the Eye of Enlightenment. This is a vision of perfect harmony and peace in the midst of the confusion of all that arises and decays. It is the appropriate antidote to the paranoia of a mind closing in upon itself for self-protection.

As these beings appear, they are also accompanied by four subsidiary aspects of their intrinsic nature. In this environment, the bodhisattvas act as regents, or representatives, of the embodiments of enlightenment and symbolize various positive qualities that can be cultivated to assist one on the path to enlightenment. Kshitigarbha, Earth Treasury, indicates the qualities of solidity, support and richness that we associate with the earth. Maitreya, Loving-Kindness, embodies the gentle kindness that nurtures and protects all beings. The goddesses are embodiments of offerings that represent the various qualities of generosity, comfort, and hospitality we may bestow upon others. Lasya symbolizes dance and creativity, while Pushpa symbolizes the beauty of nature and flowers.

If the dead person fails to respond to the help offered by these beings and flees from the white luminosity associated with this facet of enlightenment, they are in grave danger of being overcome by aversion and hatred and consequently will find themselves drawn to the paranoid torment of the hell realms.

THE PEACEFUL VISIONS OF THE THIRD DAY

HOWEVER, IT IS POSSIBLE that the deceased person will be frightened by the hook of the radiant light of compassion and flee it because of habitual pride and negative deeds, even though the guide has given him these instructions. So, on the third day, he will encounter the Blessed Ratnasambhava and his entourage as well as the path of light formed by pride which will lead him to the human realm. Once again, the guide should instruct the deceased person, calling him by name:

Listen carefully, [Name]! On this third day, the yellow luminosity of the pure earth element will shine forth. At this point, the Blessed Ratnasambhava will come from the yellow southern realm of Shrimat and appear before you. He is yellow in color and holds a wish-fulfillling gem in his hand. Seated upon a horse throne,

he embraces his consort, Mamaki.

He is accompanied by two male bodhisattvas, Akashagarbha and Samantabhadra, nd two goddesses, Mala and Dhupa.

The yellow luminosity of feeling in its natural purity, the intensely dazzling radiant and clear yellow of the awareness of sameness, will shine out from the heart of the Blessed Ratnasambhava and his consort and penetrate your heart. This light is so brilliant that you can hardly bear to look at it.

At the same time, the soft blue light associated with the human realm will also shine forth and penetrate you. Because of your habitual pride, you will then be afraid of the dazzling yellow radiant light and try to flee in terror from it. Instead, you will feel attracted and drawn to the soft blue light of the human realm.

commentary

Afraid of remaining insignificant in a universe surveyed by a smiling Akshobhya and Buddha-lochana, for whom all appearances are ultimately devoid of self, the dead person may be too proud to surrender their ego-self. If they have failed to allow themselves to merge with those beings, an antidote to their aversion will arise from their intrinsic mind. The primordial awareness of equality will dawn in the form of golden light. Just as the great earth supports all those who live, be they rich or poor, virtuous or full of sin, of high status or low, so too the compassionate awareness of equality recognizes all sentient beings as alike in their desire for happiness and their wish to avoid pain, and holds them all equally in immeasurable love.

Temporarily arising in accordance with causes and conditions, all resultant states are generated in response to the moment and soon fade away. All living beings and the entire inanimate universe are alike in this way. Nothing is permanent and nothing arises inherently from itself. Indeed, nothing substantial truly arises at all, for all things are mere passing clouds, illusions generated by the winds of karma, and they soon dissolve back into the empty space of reality from which they seemed to arise. All of us are equally upheld by the great compassion of this awareness, even though we are devoid of inherent self-existence, impermanent, and constantly frustrated in our search for happiness, .

Do not be frightened of the intensely bright clear yellow light, but recognize it as the radiant light of awareness. Try to relax and feel drawn to it with trust and devotion. If you can recognize it as the intrinsic radiance of your own primordial mind, you will dissolve inseparably into these forms and luminosity, even if you do not feel any trust or devotion, and become enlightened. If you do not recognize this as the intrinsic radiance of your own primordial mind, you should pray thus:

"This is the radiant light of the Blessed Ratnasambhava's compassion: I will go to it for refuge!". It is the Blessed Ratnasambhava coming to lead you from the terrors of this phase of death. It is the hooklike radiant light of Ratnasambhava's compassion, so put your trust in it!

Do not be attracted to the soft blue light of the human realm! It is the enticing path formed by negative deeds accumulated through your intense pride. If you are drawn to it, you will fall into the human realm and continue to experience the misery of birth, old age, sickness, and death, with no time to liberate yourself for the cycle of existence. Do not even look at it for it is a blockage to the path to liberation. Abandon all your pride! Do not be drawn to it, do not long for it! Instead, put your trust in the dazzling yellow radiant light, with intense devotion to the Blessed Ratnasambhava and his consort, repeating this prayer with me:

"When I wander through the cycle of existence driven by intense pride, may the Blessed Ratnasambhava go before me on the luminous path of the awareness of sameness, with his consort, Mamaki, behind me. May they save me from fearful dangers in the death phase and escort me to the state of perfect Enlightenment!"

By uttering this prayer with ardent trust and devotion, the deceased person will dissolve as rainbow light into the heart of Ratnasambhava and become a transfigured celestial buddha in the southern buddha-realm of Shrimat. Instructed in this way, the deceased person will certainly be liberated, no matter how feeble their abilities.

commentary

At this time, the primordial awareness of equality manifests itself in the form of Ratnasambhava, the Jewel-Born, united with his consort, Mamaki, She who is My Mother. Together, these beings represent spiritual wealth and richness. Ratnasambhava holds the mythical wish-fulfillling gem in his hand and offers it to us. This gem is the enriching jewel of perfect contentment, the nourishing aspect of enlightenment, splendidly glorious with trustworthy virtue free of any trickery or deceit. These beings are accompanied by the bodhisattvas Akashagarbha, Space Treasury, who represents a boundless richness of opportunities, and Samantabhadra, All-Good, who embodies virtuous conduct. The goddess Mala symbolizes adornments in the form of a garland, and Dhupa the pleasing fragrance of incense. If the deceased fails to respond to their inspirational assistance, their habitual pride will draw them back to the human realm they have just left with all its poverty and defects.

THE PEACEFUL VISIONS OF THE FOURTH DAY

HOWEVER, IT IS POSSIBLE that the deceased person will be frightened by the hooklike radiant light of compassion and flee it because of habitual desire and negative deeds, even though the guide has repeatedly given him these instructions. So, on the fourth day, he will encounter the Blessed Amitabha and his entourage as well as the path of light formed from desire and avarice which will lead him to the realm of the hungry ghosts. Once again, the guide should instruct the deceased person, calling him by name:

Listen carefully, [Name]! On this fourth day, the red luminosity of the pure fire element will shine forth. At this point, the Blessed Amitabha will come from the red western realm of Sukhavati and appear before you. He is red in color and holds a lotus in his hand. Seated upon a peacock throne, he embraces his consort, Pandaravasini. He is accompanied by two male bodhisattvas, Avalokiteshvara and Manjushri, and two goddesses, Gita and Aloka.

The red luminosity of ideation in its natural purity, the intensely dazzling radiant and clear red of the discriminating awareness, will shine out from the heart of the Blessed Amitabha and his consort and penetrate your heart. This light is so brilliant that you can hardly bear to look at it.

At the same time, the soft yellow light associated with the realm of hungry ghosts will also shine forth and penetrate you. Because of your habitual desire and avarice, you will then be afraid of the dazzling red radiant light and try to flee in terror from it. Instead, you will feel attracted and drawn to the soft yellow light of the realm of hungry ghosts.

commentary

Such magnificent wealth, however, may overwhelm the deceased person with its splendor. It may simply be too opulent, too full of the outpourings of generosity, so supportive that it seems suffocating, and their mind may once again turn away in fear. When this is experienced after death, the deceased person next becomes aware of the dawning of his or her own intrinsic awareness that is able to discriminate with precision. The mind is flooded with a shining redness that is all-pervading and vibrant in its intensity.

Having previously been overawed by a brief glimpse that revealed the insubstantiality of his or her own artificially constructed reality, having witnessed the manner in which all things arise from causes and conditions, and having seen that all persons and things which exist are truly no more than temporary illusions, the deceased person is now confronted by his or her own natural knowledge of true benefit and harm. This is spontaneously discriminating awareness; the awareness which easily recognizes the special potential for bliss in all beings and the uniquely useful qualities of every aspect of the material world. Effortless and entirely free of mental elaboration, this clear discriminating awareness directly perceives what is useful and what is not.

Abandon your desire and avarice! Do not be frightened of the intensely bright clear red light, but recognize it as the radiant light of awareness. Try to relax and feel drawn to it with trust and devotion. If you can recognize it as the intrinsic radiance of your own primordial mind, you will dissolve inseparably into these forms and luminosity, even if you do not feel any trust or devotion, and become enlightened. If you do not recognize this as the intrinsic radiance of your own primordial mind, you should pray thus:

"This is the radiant light of the Blessed Amitabha's compassion: I will go to it for refuge!".

It is the Blessed Amitabha coming to lead you from the terrors of this phase of death. It is the hooklike radiant light of Amitabha's compassion, so put your trust in it!

Do not be attracted to the soft yellow light of the realm of hungry ghosts! It is the path formed by negative deeds accumulated through your intense desire and avarice. If you are drawn to it, you will fall into the realm of hungry ghosts and experience unbearable sufferings of hunger and thirst.

Do not even look at it, for it is a blockage to the path to liberation. Abandon all your desire and avarice! Do not be drawn to it, do not long for it! Instead, put your trust in the dazzling red radiant light, with intense devotion to the Blessed Amitabha and his consort, repeating this prayer with me:

"When I wander through the cycle of existence driven by intense desire and avarice, may the Blessed Amitabha go before me on the luminous path of the discriminating awareness, with his consort, Pandaravasini, behind me.

May they save me from fearful dangers in the death phase and escort me to the state of perfect Enlightenment!"

By uttering this prayer with ardent trust and devotion, the deceased person will dissolve as rainbow light into the heart of Amitabha and become a transfigured celestial buddha in the western buddha-realm of Sukhavati.

commentary

At this time, the primordial awareness that discriminates precisely manifests itself in the form of Amitabha, Boundless Light, united with his consort, Pandaravasini, She Who is Clothed in White. Together these beings represent detachment from all the delightful yet delusory pleasures that people chase after during their lifetimes. Amitabha and Pandaravasini are untouched by greed and desire, anger, aversion, or mental blindness.

These beings are accompanied by the bodhisattvas Avalokiteshvara, He Who Attends to the Cries of Beings, who represents the active application of compassion, and Manjushri, the Noble Gentle One, who embodies wise conduct. The goddess Gita symbolizes creativity through song, and Aloka, the comfort of light and warmth.

If the deceased person fails to respond to their inspirational assistance, his or her habitual greed will lead him or her into the impoverished realm of the hungry ghosts.

THE PEACEFUL VISIONS OF THE FIFTH DAY

HOWEVER, IT IS POSSIBLE that the deceased person will be frightened by the hook of the radiant light of compassion and flee it because of habitual envy and negative deeds, even though the guide has repeatedly given him these instructions. So, on the fifth day, he will encounter the Blessed Amoghasiddhi and his entourage, as well as the path of light formed from jealousy which will lead him to the realm of the demi-gods. Once again, the guide should instruct the deceased person, calling him by name:

Listen carefully, [Name]! On this fifth day, the green luminosity of the pure wind element will shine forth. At this point, the Blessed Amoghasiddhi will come from the green northern realm of Prakuta and appear before you. He is green in color and holds crossed vajras in his hand. Seated upon an eagle throne, he embraces his consort, Tara. He is accompanied by two male bodhisattvas, Vajrapani and Sarvanivarana-vishkambhin, and two goddesses, Gandha and Naivedya.

The green luminosity of motivation in its natural purity, the intensely dazzling radiant and clear green of the awareness which accomplishes actions, will shine out from the heart of the Blessed Amoghasiddhi and his consort and penetrate your heart. This light is so brilliant that you can hardly bear to look at it.

At the same time, the soft red light associated with the realm of demi-gods will also shine forth and penetrate you. Because of your habitual envy and jealousy, you will then be afraid of the dazzling green radiant light and try to flee in terror from it. Instead, you will feel attracted and drawn to the soft red light of the realm of demi-gods.

commentary

If the dead person was blinded by envy and hid themselves away in order to escape the magnificence of Amitabha and his entourage, they are confronted by a further aspect of their own primordial awareness. Now the awareness which spontaneously accomplishes deeds shines forth.

Just as the previous awareness clearly discerns the potential for benefit in all situations, so this accomplishment awareness enables one to understand, intuitively, how to realize that potential through actions. Just as the awareness that precisely discriminates can recognize the ingrained inclinations and tendencies of all those it encounters, so too, the light of this new dawn shows the way in which one can successfully accomplish all things that beings need for fulfillment of their purposes, by fitting one's actions to match their various inclinations.

If we burn with the fire of anger, this awareness acts with soothing compassion. If we are weakened by material or spiritual poverty, it manifests the solidity of nourishment and gives strength through encouraging the heart. If we are afflicted by miserly greed, we are shown the liberating benefits of generosity. If we are attached to the realm of sensual pleasures, we are guided to bliss by demonstrations of unbounded freedom. And if we are afflicted by ignorance and confusion, we will have all our doubts dispelled.

Do not be frightened of the intensely bright clear green light, but recognize it as the radiant light of awareness. Try to relax and feel drawn to it with trust and devotion, praying thus: "This is the radiant light of the Blessed Amoghasiddhi's compassion: I will go to it for refuge!" It is the Blessed Amoghasiddhi coming to lead you from the terrors of this phase of death. It is the hooklike radiant light of Amoghasiddhi's compassion, so put your trust in it without any fear!

Do not be attracted to the soft red light of the realm of demi-gods! It is the enticing path formed by negative deeds accumulated through your intense envy and jealousy. If you are drawn to it, you will fall into the realm of demi-gods and experience unbearable sufferings of strife and quarrelling. Do not even look at it, for it is a blockage to the path to liberation. Abandon all your envy and jealousy! Do not be drawn to it! Instead, put your trust in the dazzling green radiant light, with intense devotion to the Blessed Amoghasiddhi and his consort, repeating this prayer with me:

"When I wander through the cycle of existence driven by intense envy and jealousy, may the Blessed Amoghasiddhi go before me on the luminous path of action-accomplishing awareness, with his consort, Tara, behind me.

May they save me from fearful dangers in the death phase and escort me to the state of perfect Enlightenment!"

By uttering this prayer with ardent trust and devotion, the deceased person will dissolve as rainbow light into the heart of Amoghasiddhi and become a transfigured celestial buddha in the northern buddha-realm of Prakuta.

commentary

At this time, the intrinsic primordial awareness which spontaneously accomplishes deeds manifests itself in the form of Amoghasiddhi, He Who Accomplishes without Fail, united with his consort, Tara, the Savioress. Together, these beings represent mastery of universal causality. They show that if this facet of enlightenment is developed, one may spontaneously solve all problems with skillful ease.

These beings are accompanied by the bodhisattvas Vajrapani, He Who Holds a Vajra in his Hand, who represents indivisible union of insight and skillfull means, and Sarvanivarana-vishkambhin, He Who Clears Away All Impurities, who embodies the ability to eliminate all obstacles and negativity through his skillfull means. The goddess Gandha symbolizes the luxuriousness of perfume, and Naivedya the comfort of food and nourishment.

But if the dead person again fails to respond to the inspirational assistance offered by this group of beings, their habitual jealousy will unfailingly draw them into the realm of the demi-gods that is ever beset with wars of envy and dissatisfaction.

THE PEACEFUL VISIONS OF THE SIXTH DAY

EVEN THOUGH THE GUIDE has repeatedly pointed out the significance of the visions in the above manner, there are those who have no previous experience of the pure visions of the five awarenesses because of their long involvement with negative tendencies. Consequently, even though the visions have been explained to them, they are dragged backward by those negative tendencies. They are terrified and alarmed by the luminosity and the radiant lights and wander away lost, not held securely by the light-hooks of compassion.

On the sixth day, the five groups of Buddhas with their consorts and entourage will appear simultaneously. At the same time, the dull luminosity of the six modes of existence will also appear simultaneously. The guide should call on the deceased person by name and instruct them with these words:

Listen carefully, [Name]! Though I explained to you the nature of the five groups of enlightened beings to you as they each appeared in turn, your previous negative tendencies caused you to become alarmed and now you are still stranded here. If you had recognized the inherent radiance of any one of the five awarenesses as your own projection, you would have dissolved as rainbow-light into one of those Buddhas and you would have become a transfigured celestial buddha. Instead, you did not recognize them for what they are, so you are still wandering lost. So now pay attention carefully! The five groups of Buddhas, as well as the four awareness merged together, will now come to escort you. You must recognize them!

commentary

The text has now presented each of the five aspects of a person's own intrinsic enlightenment in deity form together with their spiritual assistants. Their essential nature of awareness has been mentioned, as well as the way in which they are embodied as images at an intermediate spiritual level. We can experience these during our lifetime if we receive the appropriate meditational training that enables us to recognize these aspects for what they are. Otherwise we are overwhelmed by the negative and distorted aspects of these awarenesses in the form of emotions such as anger, attachment, and greed.

•

At this point of the death experience, the deceased person will now be confronted by all five groups of beings at once. Yet they are the innate radiance of their own natural mind from which there is no possibility of escape.

As the deceased's identity dissolves in the process of death, the mind is freed of its self-imposed limitations and experiences an infinite expansion. Unable to cling to the elements of personal existence – forms, feelings, perceptions, or motivations – that act as barriers keeping the consciousness constrained within "safe" limits, the natural radiance of the mind now escapes the bonds of the ego-self. Forms are now devoid of content or boundary, for the mind can pass right through them with ease. Feelings are no longer clearly pleasant or unpleasant, for all the emotions are thoroughly entangled so that all the appearances that arise in the mind are at once both wonderful and frightening. Perceptions can no longer be distinguished in terms of sound, taste, smell, and so on, for the separate organs of ear, tongue, and nose are gone and sensations simply flood the mind directly and without limit. There can be no impulse of will, for there remains nothing to cling to and it is impossible to see any direction toward any goal.

White, yellow, red, and green lights that are the
    four pure elements will shine forth.
Vairochana and his consort will come from his realm
    of Ghanavyuha and appear in the center.
    Akshobhya and his consort will come with his
    entourage from the realm of Abhirati and appear
    in the east. Ratnasambhava and his consort will
    come with his entourage from the realm of Shrimat
    and appear in the south. Amitabha and his consort
    will come with his entourage from the realm of
    Sukhavati and appear in the west. Amoghasiddhi
    and his consort will come with his entourage from
    the realm of Prakuta and appear in the north.
Stationed around these five groups of Buddhas, the
    four wrathful male and female gatekeepers will also
    appear — white Vijaya with his consort Ankusha
    in the east, yellow Yamantaka with
    his consort Pasha in the south, red Hayagriva
    with his consort Shrinkhala in the west, and
    green Amritakundali with his consort
    Ghanta in the north.
Six savior Buddhas will also appear — a white Indra
    for the gods, a green Vemacitra for the
    demi-gods, a yellow Shakyasimha for humans,
    a blue Dhruvasimha for the animals, a red
    Jvalamukha for the hungry ghosts, and a black
    Dharmaraja for the hell realms.
The All-good Father and the All-good Mother
    will also appear.

commentary

In its perfect and primordial form, our intrinsically enlightened mind can be viewed as a mandala-like structure that radiates out from the center in a clockwise direction. During the transitional phase of death, or during times of advanced creative meditation, all the limitless possibilities inherent in the basic framework of our human existence suddenly manifest together as an array of symbols which fill the sky.

Now, the full splendor of this primordial mandala shines forth, filled with various images of the aspects of enlightenment with all, their consorts and the male and female assistants of their entourage. They now appear together as an indication of the inherent unity of all things. Thus the elements of reality are united with their qualities and skillfully woven into a glorious tapestry of spontaneously liberating great compassion that reaches to the hearts of all beings.

From the heavens to the hells, the power of enlightenment reaches out to manifest in all the realms of existence and brings peaceful release from suffering. This power takes on the forms most suitable for the different types of beings with their associated negativity. Each one of this group of six Buddhas acts as a savior to his specific area of compassion, skillfully overcoming the pride of the gods, the envy of the demi-gods, the attachment of humans, the ignorance of animals, the greed of the hungry ghosts and the hatred of those in the hell realms. They show us that the compassionate power of enlightenment is ever present for our benefit if only we would avail ourselves of it.

*This array of forty-two beings will emerge from
your heart and appear before you. Recognize them
as manifestations of your own purified projections!
These realms do not exist anywhere else than in the
center and four directions of your heart.
They now come forth from your heart and appear
before you. These beings do not come from
anywhere else but are primordially formed in the
inherent energy of your own primordial mind,
so recognize them as such!
These beings are perfectly proportioned, neither too
large nor too small, each with their various
adornments, dress, and colors, as well as their
individual posture, thrones, and symbols.*

*Each of the five Buddhas embrace their consorts
and each group is encircled with a rainbow of
light. The entire mandala with all the groups of
beings in male and female forms appears complete
before you at the same time. They are your
personal deities so recognize them as such!
From the hearts of each of these five Buddhas and
their consorts, the extremely subtle and clear light
of the four awareness combined will shine like a
ribbon of sunbeams into your own heart.*

74

commentary

This mandala is an embodiment of the five aspects of intrinsic enlightenment that spreads out to encompass all beings within its boundless scope. Entrances into this mandala are located in the four directions, guarded by beings who symbolize the limitless qualities of loving-kindness, compassion, sympathetic joy, and equanimity. These four virtues act as antidotes to our most destructive and negative emotions. Loving-kindness counteracts hatred, compassion attachment, sympathetic joy envy, and equanimity pride. The gatekeepers of the mandala embody these virtues.

In the east stands Vijaya and his consort, with the hook of limitless love that captures the hearts of all beings. In the south stands Yamantaka and his consort, with the noose of limitless compassion that encircles us all. In the west stands Hayagriva and his consort, with the iron chains of limitless joy from which none can escape. Finally in the north stands Amritakundali and his consort, with the resounding bell of limitless equanimity that makes no judgmental distinctions whatsoever.

These four boundless virtues are the essential quality of the perfect mandala and the sign of this is the all-encompassing figure of the All-good Father and Mother in rapturous union. This primordial couple, representing the enlightenment that has never been lost, are naked and unadorned, as befits the original condition, and the entire mandala of peaceful deities shines forth from the utter purity and natural simplicity of their hearts.

At the time of death, people pass beyond the world of illusions. They should strive to abandon all their habitual prejudices concerning the way things are. Their attempts to cling to reality are more and more difficult to sustain as their consciousness explodes into a vast kaleidoscope of shimmering balls of light and rainbow rays.

From the heart of Vairochana, a sheet of the radiant white light, dazzling and awesome, of the awareness of the continuum of reality will shine forth into your heart. Within that sheet of radiant light there are white beads of light, extremely bright, dazzling, and awesome, like mirrors facing you. These beads of light are also adorned with five similar beads of light. Each of these is again adorned with five beads of light and so on into infinity.

From the heart of Akshobhya, a sheet of the radiant blue light of the mirror-like awareness will shine forth into your heart, adorned with azure-blue beads of light like turquoise bowls facing you. These are in turn adorned with five smaller and smaller beads of azure-blue light into infinity.

From the heart of Ratnasambhava, a sheet of the radiant yellow light of the awareness of sameness will shine forth into your heart, adorned with yellow beads of light like golden bowls facing you. These are in turn adorned with five smaller and smaller beads of yellow light into infinity.

From the heart of Amitabha, a sheet of the radiant red light of the discriminating awareness will shine forth into your heart, adorned with red beads of light like coral bowls facing you. These are in turn adorned with five smaller and smaller beads of red light into infinity.

commentary

The deceased person is now bedazzled by these spiraling lights which seem to rush toward him or her from every direction. It is a terrifying experience and the guide must do his best to reassure him or her.

The beginningless series of births and deaths are futile and all will have been in vain if a true understanding is not now accomplished. Even if the dead person has not yet accomplished anything of spiritual value, now is the time to start! If we are using this text to help the dead find their way to liberation, we should repeatedly stress the importance of this fact and do our best to prevent the deceased person from degenerating further. Attachment to his or her own sense of self-importance simply leads the deceased person from one state of misery to another and he or she must be urged to abandon such foolish conceit before his or her condition becomes even worse!

•

During our own lifetimes we should seek out a true spiritual friend from whom we may learn the way of traveling the spiritual path. Having found such a person, we should serve him or her with devotion. Having listened to his or her teachings and discerned their meaning, it is very beneficial if we retire to a solitary place and live in simplicity. We should constantly engage in meditation until true realization arises in our minds. Such a practice is good, but in this life we are easily distracted by worldly concerns and, if our perseverance is weak, the quest for knowledge of reality is difficult to see through to the end.

These sheets of light also shine forth from the inherent
energy of your own primordial mind — They come
from nowhere else, so be neither attached nor
frightened by them! Rest serenely in a state free
from judgmental thoughts. All the images of the
beings and the radiant lights will dissolve into you
and you will become an enlightened being.

You should understand that the green light of the
action-accomplishing awareness does not appear
here because the energy of your primordial mind is
still immature.

In this way, you have experienced the combined four
awarenesses, the so-called passageway of
indivisible divine insight and purity.

If at this point you can recognize them as your own
projections, you will reach the changeless path of
pure reality. You will dissolve into the being of the
great spontaneous primordial mind and become
enlightened as a transfigured celestial buddha,

never to fall back into the cycle of existence.

At the same time as the radiant lights of the
awarenesses shine forth, the impure delusive lights
of the six modes of existence will also appear — the
dull white light of gods, the dull red light of the
demi-gods, the dull blue light of humans, the dull
green light of animals, the dull yellow light of the
hungry ghosts and the dull gray light of the hell-
beings. When that happens, do not be attracted
or drawn to any of those lights, but remain relaxed
in a state free from judgmental thought.

If you are afraid of the radiant lights of the
awarenesses and are attracted to the lights of the
six impure modes of existence, you will take on a
body in one of those modes of existence.

You will experience nothing but hardship with no
chance of liberation from the great ocean of misery
in the cycle of existence.

commentary

In the transitional phase of death, however, the vision of reality is more immediate and direct and thus the result is not so difficult to attain. "Wake up, then, oh you who are now deceased! Do not waste this valuable opportunity for realization. Your own true nature is dancing as a whirling image in front of your face. Look at it! Do not hide away. Recognize it for what it is and do not be afraid. If you let this precious opportunity slip away, you will be born again under the power of habitual delusions and the chance for final release from suffering may not come again."

•

An opportunity to experience reality under the guidance of a qualified teacher is extremely rare and valuable. It is a unique and special occasion, like that of a blind man who stumbles upon a hoard of treasure. When such an opportunity has arisen, it would be foolish for us to waste it and become distracted by the outer form of the world with all its seductive images. It may be the one and only chance for all our dreams and aspirations to be realized. If we divert our attention now away from the central point, then any other accomplishments we may have will be indeed be meaningless! A knowledge of ten million facts and figures is no substitute for even a brief glimpse into the heart of reality as it really is. We must recognize the truth of impermanence and procrastinate no longer. Time wasted now will lead to unavoidable regret later. Failing to pay attention now, while the opportunity is present, is to act like a madman who drinks poison. The result is self-destruction!

If you have not had instructions from a teacher, you will be afraid of these beings and the pure lights of the awarenesses and feel attracted to the impure lights of cyclic existence. Resist this feeling and try to trust the dazzling and bright pure lights of the awarenesses. Put your trust in these lights, with the thought that these radiant lights have been sent by the Blessed Buddhas to take hold of you with their compassion. Resisting the dull lights of the six modes of existence, you should pray with one-pointed sincerity to the five Buddhas with their consorts:

"When I wander through the cycle of existence
driven by the five poisons of negativity,
may the five Buddhas go before me
on the luminous path of the four awarenesses
    combined,
with their consorts behind me.
May they save me from fearful dangers of
    the death phase
and escort me to their five pure Buddha-realms! "

Most people will recognize the nature of the visions when they have been clearly instructed in this manner and will generally be liberated.

commentary

All teachings of the Buddha are encapsulated by the four truths he taught his first disciples. First, it is important to understand the truth of suffering. The whole of existence is permeated by suffering, frustration, and dissatisfaction to such an extent that, when the pain subsides just a little, we mistakenly imagine that we are experiencing happiness. Desiring to keep the things we have, we suffer when these are taken away by thieves or force of circumstance. Thus, as a result of impermanence and change, there is suffering in loss, degeneration, break-down, and decay. Being hot, the desire for cold arises in the mind but, being cold, we wish for heat. Wishing to avoid suffering, we flee from its perceived causes but these perceptions only serve to increase anxiety so that further sufferings follow. Having little control over our circumstances, misfortunes arise despite our best efforts to keep them at bay. Even our very bodies act as a magnet for pain. Tormented by hunger, thirst, sickness, and accidental injury, no-one escapes suffering for long.

The root cause of suffering is explained as the second of the Buddha's truths. Quite simply, it is our own desire for sensual pleasure and our attachment to the objects of the senses that cause us so much pain. Being deluded concerning the reality of this world, we react to the phantoms of our perceptions with lust or anger. We are filled with desire or hatred, pride or jealousy, and all such conceits cause us to act in a way that gives pain to ourselves and others. By habitually interacting with the world thus, we develop a tendency to maintain the causes of sorrow from one life to the next so that there seems no escape.

But the third truth teaches us that there is the possibility of release. And the fourth truth outlines the structure of the path to release from suffering through a structured program of morality, insight, and meditation.

THE VISIONS OF THE SEVENTH DAY

HOWEVER, THERE ARE some unfortunate types of people who had no spiritual training, who lived in backward places, or who were corrupt in their spiritual practice. They are led astray by their previous actions and wander lost downwards even when they have been instructed during this phase of death.

On the seventh day, a group of stern *vidyadharas* with their entourage will come from the pure sky realm to escort the deceased person. At the same time, the dull green light, formed by ignorance, leading to the animal realm will appear. Once again, the guide should instruct the deceased person, calling him by name:

Listen carefully, [Name]! On the seventh day, a pure multicolored radiant light of purified negative propensities will shine forth and then a host of vidyadhara *deities will come from the pure sky realm to escort you.*

In the middle of a mandala enveloped in light and rainbows, the supreme vidyadhara of maturation, the red Lotus Lord of Dance, will appear. His body shines with the five colors and he embraces intimately his red dakini *consort. They dance holding curved knives and blood-filled skull cups, gazing up at the sky.*

commentary

During their lifetime, the deceased may have been fortunate enough to encounter true spiritual friends but so often their words are ignored. At this stage of the death experience, the symbolic forms of teachers appear to the dead as tantric masters with stern looks on their faces. The dead will not see again the peaceful images of the Buddhas in their benign aspect. They have come to remind the deceased person of all the teachings that they may have received during their lifetime and to admonish them for being so sluggish in their attainment of liberation.

Dressed in the clothing of wild, heroic yogins, and carrying the attributes of those who practice in the fearful charnel grounds of ancient India, these tantric teachers are divinely inspired sages whose dances of liberation are an ecstatic display of the power of truth itself. Upon their heads they wear crowns of five skulls, showing that they have been blessed by the five Buddhas. Their earrings indicate that their ears are constantly adorned with the sound of religious teachings and the necklaces on their throats show that the truth is all they speak. Bracelets and bangles upon their arms show the power of their enlightened deeds, and girdles of bone hanging down like aprons indicate the keeping of pure vows. They wear skirts of tiger skin to indicate their control of the senses and their mastery of all emotional states. Playing music on drums fashioned from human skulls and trumpets of thigh-bone indicates their awareness of impermanence and the selfless nature of all phenomena. Waving flags of human skin indicates that they have stripped away the veils of illusion and their playful attitude to death indicates total transcendence of the worldly sphere. Satisfying their thirst with blood drunk from skull cups, they show that they are free of any desire. The sharp knives they wield cut away wrong views at a single stroke.

*In the east of the mandala, the vidyadhara called
  He Who Abides on the Levels will appear.
  His body is white in color and he has a smiling face.
  He intimately embraces his white dakini consort,
  and they dance holding curved knives and
  blood-filled skull cups, gazing up at the sky.
In the south of the mandala, the vidyadhara called
  He Who has Mastery of Life will appear. His body
  is yellow in color and he has a smiling face.
  He intimately embraces his yellow dakini consort,
  and they dance holding curved knives and
  blood-filled skull cups, gazing up at the sky.
In the west of the mandala, the vidyadhara called the
  Great Seal will appear. His body is red in color and
  with a smiling face. He intimately embraces his red
  dakini consort, and they dance holding curved knives
  and blood-filled skull cups, gazing up at the sky.
In the north of the mandala, the vidyadhara called
  Spontaneous Accomplishment will appear.
  His body is green in color and he has a stern face.
  He intimately embraces his green dakini consort,
  and they dance holding curved knives
  and blood-filled skull cups, gazing up at the sky.
All around these vidyadharas there will appear countless
  hosts of dakinis from all the cemeteries and places of
  pilgrimage, together with all the protectors of religion.
  They wear bone ornaments and carry drums, thigh-
  bone trumpets, skull-drums, banners, ribbons and
  pennants made from human skin, and incense made
  from burnt human flesh. Dancing, accompanied by
  countless types of musical instruments, they pulsate,
  sway and tremble, filling all the realms of the universe
  as if to make your head split apart. They come to
  escort those who have upheld their religious
  commitments and to punish those who have not.*

commentary

Renowned as "Holders of Awareness" (*vidyadhara*), these tantric masters are of five classes, corresponding to the five traditional stages of the Buddhist path to enlightenment. To begin with, there is the path of accumulation of merit. At this stage, a beginner prepares for religious practice by turning the mind towards virtue. This lays down the foundations and develops the necessary good qualities so that we may actually meet with a spiritual friend or teacher. Next is the path of connection, during which we begin to engage in the deeper teachings received from our teachers. As a result of applying ourselves to these practices, we attain the path of insight. On this level, the deeper significance of all that we have been taught becomes clearly understood. We no longer merely amuse ourselves with the words and outer forms of religion, but truly understand their meaning. Then we enter the path of meditation. In this fourth stage, the understanding we have previously gained is integrated with the mind-stream so that there remains no separation between theory and practice. When all that we have realized has become the very basis of our being, we have gained the fifth and final path of no more learning. The hallmarks of this final stage are a natural spontaneity and joyful freedom.

From the hearts of the vidyadharas, the spontaneous awareness that is purified negativity will shine forth, with five blinding radiant and dazzling lights like cords of colored threads twisted together, and penetrate your heart. At the same time, the dull green light of the animals will appear. Due to your own deluding propensities, you will be frightened by the five-colored lights and try to flee. You will find the dull green light of the animals to be attractive so do not fear the dazzling five-colored lights but recognize them as awareness.

From the midst of the radiant light, the intrinsic sound of truth will resound like the rumble of a thousand thunderclaps. It reverberates fiercely, tumultuously, with the intense sound of wrathful mantras. Do not fear it! Do not try to flee it!

Recognize it as the energy of your own primordial mind, of your own projections.

Do not become attracted to that dull green light of the animals. If you are drawn to it, you will fall into the ignorant animal realm and experience the boundless miseries of stupidity, dumbness and enslavement. Do not be drawn to that realm, for then you will have no chance of escape.

commentary

These five naturally spontaneous *vidyadharas* are associated with the attainment of the five aspects through which enlightenment, or buddhahood, is manifested. Due to their realization of the ultimate truth of openness, they manifest as awareness in wisdom itself. This vast and profound understanding is known as the embodiment of truth. It is the utter perfection of consciousness and is properly understood only by those who have attained it.

Spontaneously radiating the great compassion that effortlessly communicates itself to spiritual beings on the path of insight, they also possess bodies of light known as "joyful communication." This is the embodiment of speech. When Buddhas and bodhisattvas meet together in the realm of joy, they naturally relate to one another by means of these bodies of joyful communication.

In the realm of sentient beings, however, these beings appear in the guise of human teachers formed of flesh and blood, and this is known as the body of manifestation.

Its outer form is visible to all and indeed it may appear to some that there is nothing special about it at all. This is not to say, however, that such a body is really unimportant. Having broken the chains that bind them to the cycle of existence, enlightened beings assume physical forms on earth only for the benefit of others.

Since their bodies are born as the result of their compassionate aspirations, their birth is often accompanied by miraculous signs, and there are special marks upon their bodies. It is said that the body of a buddha possesses thirty-two major marks and eighty minor signs, each one of which is an indication of some particular aspect of his greatness. These signs are clearly visible to sages, but ordinary people may see a buddha as an ordinary human. Inwardly, however, these beings possess a body known as the integrated embodiment of their own inherent nature, because their body, speech, and mind are perfectly integrated into a harmonious whole. Because this is pervaded by joyful understanding, they are also said to have bodies of great bliss. These are the five bodies of buddhahood.

*P*ut your trust in that radiant dazzling five-colored
light and focus your attention solely upon the host
of blessed vidyadhara deities, thinking "These
vidyadharas have come with the heroes and
dakinis to escort me to the pure realm of the sky.
May they think of beings such as myself who
have not accumulated much merit or insight.
Have pity on people like me who have not been
seized by the radiant light of compassion
emanating from the five groups of Buddhas who
have appeared up until now! Do not let me sink
any lower now, you crowds of vidyadharas, but
take hold of me with your hooks of compassion!
Pull me straight up to the pure realm of the sky!"
Then you should pray thus with great sincerity:

"Think of me, you host of vidyadharas, lead me
along the path with your great kindness!
When I wander through the cycle of existence
driven by my powerful negative propensities,
may the vidyadharas go before me on the
luminous path of spontaneous awareness,
with their dakini consorts behind me.
May they save me from fearful dangers of the death
phase and escort me to the pure realm of space!"

By uttering this prayer with ardent trust and
devotion, the deceased person will dissolve as
rainbow light into the heart of the host of
vidyadharas and definitely be born in the pure
realm of space.

commentary

The dancing *vidyadhara* teachers who appear on the seventh day do not radiate from the heart of the deceased person in the same way that the previous host of peaceful deities radiated from the heart. The mandala of peaceful Buddhas was the natural manifestation of the heart-mind of the deceased person. With the final separation of consciousness from the body, however, these peaceful visions came to an end.

Soon, the corpse itself will begin to decay and dissolve. With the dissolution of gross outer matter, there will arise the terrifying forms of the wrathful deities from their home in the brain.

Now, on the seventh day, during the short transitional space between the dissolution of the mind of the deceased and the dissolution of his or her body, the memory arises of whatever religious instruction they have received, in the form of a mandala of divine teachers arising from his or her throat. The seeds of this manifestation are implanted in the throat center of speech by the wise teachers that were encountered during their lifetime. Now, during the phase of death, the memory of these wise and compassionate teachers arises, and the deceased person is once more offered the chance to connect to this visual display arising from their own intrinsic awareness and, thus, attain final release from sorrow.

THE WRATHFUL VISIONS OF THE EIGHTH DAY

UP TO NOW the deceased person has experienced seven stages of the death phase that is fraught with dangers. By having been given instructions concerning each of these stages in due sequence, countless deceased people will have recognized one or other of these stages and been liberated. Despite this, there are many types of people, some of whom have much negative karma, who carry a burden of evil deeds and who have well-ingrained negative propensities. This cycle of existence driven by the delusions of ignorance continues unabated, so there are very many people who are not liberated, but wander on downward even though they have been given these instructions in detail.

After the host of peaceful beings and the *vidyadharas* with the *dakinis* have appeared, they are transformed and reappear as the host of fifty-eight wrathful blood-drinking beings. They are different now, for this is the phase of death associated with the wrathful beings, so the deceased person will be overcome by terror, fear and panic. It will also be difficult for him to recognize anything now. He will lose control of his rationality and feel faint and dizzy. Nevertheless, liberation is easy if he is able to achieve even a little understanding of his experiences. This is because his mind becomes very focussed – he will be so terrified by the fearsome visions, his attention will have no time to wander.

commentary

During the first six days of death, the gross, outer aspects of mind gradually dissolve and produce the forty-two peaceful deities who embody facets of one's intrinsically enlightened mind, arising in stages from their center in the heart. On the next day, the subtle, inner aspects of the mind dissolve, giving rise to the appearance of the *vidyadhara* teachers and their entourage, appearing from the speech center in the throat. Then the subtle, innermost aspects of mind begin to dissolve, and give rise to the visions of the fifty-eight wrathful blood-drinking deities who appear from their center in the top of the head.

At this level of dissolution, as body and mind are fast decaying and there is almost nothing left of the former personality to cling to, the ego-self goes into a state of intense paranoia. Formerly, it held firm to the mistaken belief that itself and its world were permanent, stable entities. Now, however, all basis for that belief has been destroyed through the process of death, and the ego experiences overwhelming fear and panic in the form of terrifying hallucinations. Always fearful of being caught out, this false ego-self has had to struggle constantly to maintain its conceit in the face of the natural openness of the world. The forces of nature have always run counter to it and this is why so many people seek to conquer nature and strive to overthrow its rule. In order to protect their fragile egos, they have no wish to cooperate with nature and live with it in harmony and peace. Instead, they choose to fight against it and subjugate nature to the rule of ego.

SO NOW THE GUIDE should call to the deceased person three times and give him these instructions:

Listen carefully, [Name]! Though the peaceful beings have already appeared to you, you were unable to recognize them for what they are. You have now wandered on to this phase of the death experience. From this eighth day onwards, a host of wrathful blood-drinking beings will appear. Try to recognize them without any distractions!

The great glorious Buddha Heruka will emerge from the middle of your head and appear before you distinctly. His body is dark maroon in color, with three heads, six arms, and four outspread legs. He has three faces: the right face is white, the left one is red, and the one in the middle is dark maroon in color. The whole of his body blazes in a mass of light rays, with his nine eyes glaring terrifyingly at you. His eyebrows glint like lightning, and his teeth gleam like shining copper. He roars with boisterous laughter and makes loud hissing noises. His tawny hair blazes upward and his head is adorned with a crown of skulls and the sun and moon. His body is garlanded with black snakes and a string of freshly severed heads.

His uppermost right hand holds a wheel, the second an axe, and the third a sword. His uppermost left hand holds a bell, the second a plowshare, and the third a skull cup.

His consort Buddha-Krodheshvari is entwined about him, clasping him around the neck with her right hand and holding to his mouth a skull brimming with blood with her left hand. She makes roaring noises like thunder and ominously clucks her tongue.

Both of these beings emit great flames of awareness from the incandescent hairs on their bodies. They stand like warriors upon a throne upheld by great eagle-like garudas.

Do not be afraid of them, do not be terrified by them! Recognize them as embodiments of your own primordial mind! Do not be confused, for he is merely your own archetypal deity! There is nothing to fear, for they are really the Blessed Vairochana and his consort. You will be liberated the moment you recognize them for what they are.

When the guide reads this to the deceased person, he will recognize these beings as his own archetypal deity and merge inseparably with them, becoming a transfigured celestial Buddha.

commentary

Our ego, which assumes itself to be the most important and true thing in the world is, in fact, a mere fiction created by desire. It has no solidity of its own and demands constant attention in order to maintain its illusory status. Making a slave of its creator, it seeks to assert its false validity by dominating everything else. Thus it demands that the entire world be seen in terms of "me me me" and "mine mine mine." Anything that falls outside this scope is viewed with suspicion, mistrust, jealousy, and hatred.

At this stage of the death experience, the five groups of previously peaceful beings, embodiments of the five facets of enlightenment mentioned earlier, take on the distorted and ugly appearance of the ego itself. Though they seem to arise independently, they are actually formed from the ingrained negative energy of the deceased person.

THE WRATHFUL VISIONS OF THE NINTH DAY

YET THE DECEASED person may not recognize them and flee in terror, so then, on the ninth day, the blood-drinking Vajra Heruka will come forth to invite the deceased person. The guide should again instruct the deceased person thus:

Listen carefully, [Name]! On the ninth day, the Blessed Vajra Heruka will emerge from the eastern direction of your head and appear before you. His body is dark blue in color, with three heads, six arms, and four outspread legs. He has three faces: the right face is white, the left one is red, and the one in the middle is dark blue in color. His uppermost right hand holds a vajra, the second a skull cup, and the third an axe. His uppermost left hand holds a bell, the second a skull cup, and the third a plowshare.

His consort Vajra-Krodheshvari is entwined about him, clasping him around the neck with her right hand and holding to his mouth a skull brimming with blood with her left hand.

Do not be afraid of them; do not be terrified by them! Recognize them as embodiments of your own primordial mind! Do not be confused for he is merely your own archetypal deity! There is nothing to fear for they are really the Blessed Akshobhya and his consort. You will be liberated the moment you recognize them for what they are.

When the guide reads this to the deceased person, he will recognize these beings as his own archetypal deity and merge inseparably with them, becoming a transfigured celestial Buddha.

commentary

These images of wrathful beings may seem at first sight to be similar to the devils and demons familiar to us in the West, but they are actually quite different and certainly neither evil nor to be feared once they have been recognized. They are, in fact, the way in which our intrinsic enlightenment tries to shock us out of our complacency by showing us the ugly and terrifying nature of our ego-self.

To understand the symbolism involved here, we must be familiar with the legend that underlies these wrathful images. Once, in an age long passed, there were two friends who went together to study religion at the feet of a master. When it was explained to them both that the essence of innermost reality is truly spontaneous awareness, they each went off separately to practice what they had been taught. One of them relaxed his mind through meditation and yoga and allowed all negative emotions to simply float away like clouds in the sky until his consciousness was clear, open, and bright. The other began to assert his ego through murder and theft. Using his skill and intelligence to organize a criminal network, he quickly set up a chain of brothels and gambling houses so that he became very rich and powerful indeed.

When the two friends met again some time later, each was surprised to see how the other had understood the teachings they had received together. Returning to the teacher for advice about who was right and who was wrong, they were told that the goal of freedom is freedom from the ego. Hearing this, the one who had spent so much time and energy boosting his ego became very angry indeed and killed the master on the spot. Consequently, in subsequent incarnations, the student who was dominated by the evil ego was born repeatedly in the form of various wild animals and fell down into the lowest of the hell-realms.

THE WRATHFUL VISIONS OF THE TENTH DAY

YET THERE ARE SOME who are greatly enshrouded by their negative actions and flee, failing to recognize these beings for what they are, so then on the tenth day the blood-drinking Ratna Heruka will come forth to invite the deceased person. The guide should again instruct the deceased person thus:

Listen carefully, [Name]! On the tenth day the Blessed Ratna Heruka will emerge from the southern direction of your head and appear before you. His body is dark yellow in color, with three heads, six arms, and four outspread legs. He has three faces: the right face is white, the left one is red, and the one in the middle is dark yellow in color. His uppermost right hand holds a jewel, the second a spear with three impaled heads, and the third a club. His uppermost left hand holds a bell, the second a skull cup, and the third a trident.

His consort Ratna-Krodheshvari is entwined about him, clasping him around the neck with her right hand and holding to his mouth a skull brimming with blood with her left hand.

Do not be afraid of them; do not be terrified by them! Recognize them as embodiments of your own primordial mind! Do not be confused for he is merely your own archetypal deity! There is nothing to fear for they are really the Blessed Ratnasambhava and his consort. You will be liberated the moment you recognize them for what they are.

When the guide reads this to the deceased person, he will recognize these beings as his own archetypal deity and merge inseparably with them, becoming a transfigured celestial Buddha.

commentary

As the student's burden of negative karma lessened somewhat, he was able to be born as the illegitimate son of a prostitute. Since his limbs were coarse and rough, his mother died as he passed through the birth canal. Both the mother's corpse and the infant were taken to the charnel ground and left there. The child drank milk from the breasts of his mother's corpse and then sucked at the yellow fluid that oozed out. After that, he ate the breasts themselves and thus sustained himself for seven days. Then, opening up the chest cavity, he consumed her lungs and heart. After that, he ate the rest of her flesh. When the mother had been completely consumed, knowing that there was no more to be had, he went off and ate other corpses. Sustaining himself in this way, the hair on his body grew up like bristles and his nails were like iron hooks. Wings sprouted from his back and, knowing how to fly, he went everywhere, up and down, killing beings and eating them. Known by the name of Rudra, he was proclaimed the most fearful of all living creatures. In this form, he became the ultimate embodiment of the stupidity, cruelty, and greed of the ego-self.

THE WRATHFUL VISIONS OF THE ELEVENTH DAY

YET THERE ARE SOME people who fail to recognize these beings for what they are, even though they have been instructed in this way, but who are weighed down by their negative tendencies and flee in terror. So then, on the eleventh day, the blood-drinking Padma Heruka will come forth to invite the deceased person. The guide should again instruct the deceased person thus:

Listen carefully, [Name]! On the eleventh day, the Blessed Padma Heruka will emerge from the western direction of your head and appear before you. His body is dark red in color, with three heads, six arms, and four outspread legs. He has three faces: the right face is white, the left one is red, and the one in the middle is dark red in color. His uppermost right hand holds a lotus, the second a spear with three impaled heads, and the third a staff. His uppermost left hand holds a bell,

the second a blood-filled skull cup, and the third a small drum.

His consort Padma-Krodheshvari is entwined about him, clasping him around the neck with her right hand and holding to his mouth a skull brimming with blood with her left hand.

Do not be afraid of them; do not be terrified by them! Recognize them as embodiments of your own primordial mind! Do not be confused for he is merely your own archetypal deity! There is nothing to fear for they are really the Blessed Amitabha and his consort. You will be liberated the moment you recognize them for what they are.

When the guide reads this to the deceased person, he will recognize these beings as his own archetypal deity and merge inseparably with them, becoming a transfigured celestial Buddha.

commentary

Rudra's horrific manifestation of the ego-self was finally destroyed by the power of enlightenment; the Buddhas themselves took on Rudra's violently ugly form, transforming it into a symbol of compassionate awareness. The purpose of this was to show that enlightenment and compassion can overcome all evil and darkness. Even the most disgusting ego-self can eventually be redeemed.

Because the body of the ego-monster Rudra in his final birth had three faces, six arms and four legs, the Heruka Buddhas appear likewise. Each of the five Herukas has a different color as the text mentions. These represent the same five awareness qualities of the primordially pure mind that were described earlier when the peaceful beings were making their appearance. These wrathful beings have ferocious white faces on the right sides of their heads that destroy the afflictions of anger. The left red face annihilates all impurities of desire, and the central face of the family color vanquishes ignorance. Each face has an unblinking third eye in the center of the forehead so that none of these mental defilements may pass by unnoticed. Thus their three faces indicate the destruction of the three basic forms of negativity.

Their six arms show the ability to liberate beings from the six realms of existence, and their four legs symbolize the four modes of magical activity as well as the liberation of beings from the four kinds of birth: from eggs, wombs, moisture, and miraculously. Simultaneously, they trample down upon the four qualities of demonic influence: confusion of mind, attachment to the body, death, and conceit.

The drinking of blood from a skull indicates that their awareness consumes all falsehood, and the weapons that they brandish in their hands destroy all opposition.

THE WRATHFUL VISIONS OF THE TWELFTH DAY

YET THERE ARE SOME people who still fail to recognize these beings for what they are, even though they have been instructed in this way, but who are weighed down by their negative tendencies and flee in terror. So then, on the twelfth day, the blood-drinking Karma Heruka will come forth to invite the deceased person, followed by the Maidens, the Witches, and the Ladies. The guide should again instruct the deceased person thus:

Listen carefully, [Name]! On the twelfth day, the Blessed Karma Heruka will emerge from the northern direction of your head and appear before you. His body is dark green in color, with three heads, six arms, and four outspread legs. He has three faces: the right face is white, the left one is red, and the one in the middle is dark green in color. His uppermost right hand holds a sword, the second a spear with three impaled heads, and the third a staff. His uppermost left hand holds a bell, the second a skull cup, and the third a plowshare.

His consort Karma-Krodheshvari is entwined about him, clasping him around the neck with her right hand and holding to his mouth a skull brimming with blood with her left hand.

Do not be afraid of them; do not be terrified by them! Recognize them as embodiments of your own primordial mind! Do not be confused for he is merely your own archetypal deity! There is nothing to fear for they are really the Blessed Amoghasiddhi and his consort. You will be liberated the moment you recognize them for what they are.

When the guide reads this to the deceased person, he will recognize these beings as his own archetypal deity and merge inseparably with them, becoming a transfigured celestial Buddha.

commentary

These Heruka Buddhas are invariably dressed in the "spoils of war": the grisly clothes and ornaments of the charnel ground that were originally stripped from the body of the defeated Rudra, and have been subsequently worn by all the wrathful manifestations of enlightenment. Their clothing includes a cloak of human skin as a sign that the ego has been stripped bare; a cloak of elephant skin symbolizing the perfection of the great path of buddhahood; and a skirt of tiger skin indicating control of the passions. Among their ornaments are the necklace, earrings, bracelets, apron, and hair net made of bone, associated with the five groups of Buddhas. Numerous snakes encircle their limbs and body, and they each wear a crown of five dry skulls, a necklace of fifty freshly severed heads, a belt of splintered bones, and so on. The sun and moon worn in their hair show the simultaneity of awareness and compassion; their protruding fangs demonstrate the annihilation of birth and death; their great wings symbolize the fulfillment of all wishes; their upraised hair shows the reversal of worldly tendencies; and their aura of flames burns up malevolent forces. They paint their faces with three ointments: the dust of human ashes on the forehead, drops of blood upon the cheeks, and a smear of fat across the chin. They dance in a manner which is both alluring and repulsive, and their dwelling is a gruesome palace made of skulls.

THE EIGHT MAIDENS

HOWEVER, THERE ARE SOME people who will turn away from these beings and go on to wander lost in the cycle of existence. The eight Maidens and the eight animal-headed Witches will emerge from within the deceased person's brain and appear to him. The guide should instruct the deceased person thus:

Listen carefully, [Name]! Eight Maidens will emerge
  from your brain and appear before you.
  Do not be afraid of them!
A white Gauri will appear from the east.
  She holds a corpse as a club in her right hand
  and a blood-filled skull cup in her left hand.
A yellow Chauri will appear from the south.
  She holds a drawn bow to shoot an arrow.
A red Pramoha will appear from the west.
  She holds a crocodile skin banner.
A black Vetali will appear from the north. She holds
  a vajra and a blood-filled skull cup in her hands.
An orange Pukkasi will appear from the south-east.
  She holds coils of intestines in her right hand and
  feeds herself with them with her left hand.
A dark green Ghasmari will appear from the south-
  west. She holds a blood-filled skull cup in her right
  hand, stirring it with a vajra in her left hand as
  she drinks it.
A pale yellow Chandali will appear from the north-
  west. She rips apart a corpse, holding its heart in
  her right hand while she chews at the corpse with
  her left hand.
A dark blue Shmashani will appear from the
  north-east. She eats a corpse which she has
  torn head from body.
These eight Maidens from the eight directions will
  emerge from your brain and place themselves
  around the five blood-drinking Herukas.
  Do not be afraid of them!

commentary

As their entourage, the Heruka Buddhas are accompanied by a fearful retinue of shape-shifting witches that appear in the guise of frenzied women. These figures have much in common with the maenads of ancient Greek religion. They are euphemistically called "Maidens" and "Ladies." These repulsive females represent the wild, untamed aspects of the natural world. Formerly they acted as attendants of Rudra but now they appear as symbols of feminine awareness.

Holding a corpse indicates holding the body free of ego, and the skull full of blood is the essence of life itself. This symbolizes passion transformed into compassion. Holding a bow and arrow represents the possession of a sharply focussed mind that is poised, ready to pierce the heart of dullness and stupidity. Crocodiles are the fearful monsters of the ocean of existence and, when this has been crossed, their skins may be waved as banners of victory. Vajras symbolize unchangeable awareness and this is to be held together with the blood of concern for the welfare of all beings. Coils of intestines represent the inner nature of transmutation and change. Hollow and insubstantial on the inside, all cycles of rebirth are mere illusions brought about by the process of cause and effect, and are no more than temporary transformations. Severing the head or heart from the corpse of egoless existence shows control of the body and its functions.

THE EIGHT WITCHES

✳

Listen carefully, [Name]! Then eight Witches from the sacred places will emerge and appear before you.

A dark maroon lion-headed Simhamukha will appear from the east. She has her arms crossed over her chest and chews a corpse in her mouth while tossing her mane.

A red tiger-headed Vyaghrimukha will appear from the south. She has her arms crossed downward, while glaring and snarling.

A black fox-head Shrigalamukha will appear from the west. She holds a razor in her right hand and intestines in her left hand which she feeds into her mouth, licking the blood.

A dark blue wolf-headed Shvanamukha will appear from the north. She holds a corpse up to her mouth with both hands, with her eyes glaring.

A pale yellow vulture-headed Gridhramukha will appear from the south-east. She carries a corpse over her shoulder and holds a skeleton in her hand.

A dark red hawk-headed Kankamukha will appear from the south-west. She carries a flayed human skin over her shoulders.

A black crow-headed Kakamukha will appear from the north-west. She holds a blood-filled skull cup in her left hand and a sword in her right hand while she gnaws a human heart and lungs.

A dark blue owl-headed Ulumukha will appear from the north-east. She eats while holding a vajra in her right hand and a sword in her left hand.

These eight Witches from sacred places will emerge from your brain and place themselves around the five blood-drinking Herukas.

Do not be afraid of them! Recognize whatever appears as the natural projection of your primordial mind's creative energy!

commentary

The sacred places of pilgrimage in this world are the cities of corruption in all directions that were formerly ruled by Rudra and his followers. Having been overthrown by the compassionate enlightenment of the Buddhas, they are now abodes of awareness in the north, south, east, west, and intermediate directions. From these places come the animal-headed messengers of Rudra that appear fearsome only to those who still cling to the ego.

Snarling and showing their teeth, these beast-women serve to remind the virtuous of the unsatisfactory nature of being born in the cycle of existence. Their wicked laughter and obscene words and gestures express the truth of worldly rebirth. Glaring with bulging eyes, they demonstrate the pure vision of primordial awareness. Rolling their eyes to the top of the head puts an end to deceptive appearances, and staring downward they show their total control over the mind and vital energies.

Since beginningless time, each of us has been born again and again, never achieving any satisfaction. The bodies of those former lives are numerous enough to fill the whole earth and the bones alone, if collected together and piled up high, would form a mountain larger than any now known. Even the blood of those former lives is sufficient to fill an ocean. Thus the eight Witches come from the sacred places bearing tokens of our futile past existences. Holding aloft the flesh of ignorance, the bones of anger and the blood of desire, they make mockery of our waste, and bring us the sharp weapons of awareness with which to cut through the bonds that tie us to an endless repetition of such meaningless misery. Recognize them for what they are and be freed!

THE FOUR GATEKEEPERS

※

Listen! Now the four gatekeepers will also emerge from your brain and appear before you. Recognize them for what they are!

A white horse-headed Ankusha will appear before you from the east. She holds an iron crook and a blood-filled skull cup in her hands.

A yellow sow-headed Pasha will appear before you from the south. She holds a noose in her hand.

A red lion-headed Shrinkhala will appear before you from the west. She holds an iron chain in her hand.

A green serpent-headed Ghanta will appear before you from the north. She holds a bell in her hand.

These four gatekeepers will emerge from your brain and appear before you: recognize them as your own archetypal deities.

commentary

Four guards now appear at the inner gates of the mandala to the east, south, west, and north. With an iron crook, she in the east, who represents boundless love, hooks all beings by the heart. She in the south, who represents boundless compassion, now draws all beings closer with her noose of compassion. In the west, she with an iron chain of boundless joy binds the hearts of all beings with gladness in virtue. And she in the north, who represents boundless equanimity, rings her bell of total equality, free of any bias or personal preference. These are the fearsome goddesses whose domains we must cross in order to reach the heart of enlightenment at the mandala center.

The dancing areas of these four goddesses in the four directions are the colors of the four elements: the white of water, the yellow of earth, the red of fire, and the green of wind.

When sickness arises, the elements are out of harmony, and disease and troubles spread, it is traditional to perform rites of pacification in the white, eastern quarter. In the realm of boundless love, all disturbances are peacefully brought to rest and all disruptions healed. Whatever has risen up in anger is pacified in the east.

When good qualities are insufficient and strength is weak, rites of enrichment may be performed in the south. In the area of great compassion, what is feeble is enhanced and made strong. Health, wealth, and strength are increased, and doubt and despair are replaced by encouragement, hope, and good will.

When things seem to have gotten out of order and chaos ensues, rites of control may be performed in the red, passionate quarter of the west. Boundless joy in all that is beneficial acts as a magnet that attracts to itself more joy and bliss. Thus, there arises an accumulation of positive energy that may be utilized for the benefit of all beings in the great mandala of the Buddha's enlightenment.

But when enemies arise that cannot be tamed by peaceful methods, the wrathful rites of extermination may be performed in the dark northern quarter to bring an end to strife. When there is nothing of a positive nature that can be brought under control, it must be destroyed. This fearful act is the ultimate weapon of the enlightened against the poison of ego. It is the very death of the self.

THE TWENTY-EIGHT LADIES

Listen carefully! The twenty-eight Ladies will now
emerge from your brain and appear before you.
They have various animal heads and carry
various implements. Do not be afraid of them!
Recognize whatever appears as the natural
projection of your primordial mind's
creative energy!

First, the six Ladies of the east will emerge from
your brain and appear before you:
a dark maroon yak-headed Rakshasi,
holding a vajra;
an orange serpent-headed Brahmi, holding a lotus;
a dark-green leopard-headed Mahadevi,
holding a trident;
a blue mongoose-headed Lobha, holding a wheel;
a red yellow-bear-headed Kumari, holding a spear;
and a white bear-headed Indrani, holding a
noose of intestines.
Do not be afraid of them!

Then, the six Ladies of the south will emerge from
your brain and appear before you:
a yellow sow-headed Vajra, holding a razor;
a red crocodile-headed Shanti, holding a jar;
a red scorpion-headed Amrita, holding a lotus;
a white hawk-headed Chandra, holding a vajra;
a dark green fox-headed Danda, holding a club;
and a dark yellow tiger-headed Rakshasi, holding
a blood-filled skull cup.
Do not be afraid of them!

Then, the six Ladies of the west will emerge from your
brain and appear before you:
a dark green vulture-headed Bakshini, holding a club;
a red horse-headed Rati, holding a human torso;
a white garuda-headed Mahabala, holding a club;
a red dog-headed Rakshasi, holding a vajra razor;
a red hoopoe-headed Kama, drawing a bow;
and a dark green deer-headed Vasuraksha,
holding a jar.
Do not be afraid of them!

Then, the six Ladies of the north will emerge from
your brain and appear before you:
a blue wolf-headed Vayudevi, holding a banner;
a red ibex-headed Nari, holding a stake;
a black sow-headed Varahi, holding a noose of teeth;
a red crow-headed Vajra, holding the skin of a child;
a dark green elephant-headed Mahahastini, holding
a human corpse;
and a blue serpent-headed Varunadevi, holding a
snake-noose.
Do not be afraid of them!

commentary

In order that we all may safely be led into the heart of the mandala that is primordial awareness itself, the first group of the twenty-eight powerful Ladies bear various symbols of fearlessness from the four quarters: the indestructible vajra and the beautiful lotus of perfect compassion, the sharp-pronged trident that simultaneously pierces through ignorance, aggression, and lust, the razor-edged discus, the spear of single-pointed penetrative awareness and the rope of illusory intestines: these come from the east. The razor that severs deceit and the jar of divine ambrosia, the club that smashes wrong views and the skull cup filled with the blood of desire: these come from the south. The headless corpse of non-ego and the bow and arrow of united insight and means: these come from the west. The banner of victory, the demon-transfixing stake, the sharp teeth that cut through aggression, the flayed skin of newly-born error and the snakes of malice: these come from the north.

Then, the four outer gatekeepers will emerge from
your brain and appear before you.
A white cuckoo-headed Vajra, holding an iron crook,
will appear before you from the east.
A yellow goat-headed Vajra, holding a noose, will
appear before you from the south.
A red lion-headed Vajra, holding an iron chain, will
appear before you from the west.
A dark green serpent-headed Vajra, holding a bell,
will appear before you from the north.

These twenty-eight Ladies arise spontaneously from
the creative energy of the fearsome Herukas:
recognize them for what they are!

When this crowd of fifty-eight blood-drinking beings
emerge from your brain and appear before you,
recognize them for what they are. If you
understand that whatever appears to you just
arises from the natural glowing energy of
your primordial mind, you will immediately
become enlightened, merged inseparably from
the blood-drinking beings.

commentary

The final members of the group of twenty-eight powerful Ladies guard the doors of the outer circle with the symbolic implements of boundless love, compassion, sympathetic joy and equanimity. These four boundless states of mind are truly the doorways to any level of spiritual realization, and thus they reappear as both the outer doorways and the inner. They are also present in both the peaceful circle and the wrathful one.

Naturally, all these visions appear utterly terrifying to those who have little awareness of their true significance. Those who have spent innumerable lifetimes believing in the reality of the outer world, and who are thus unaccustomed to the vibrancy and brilliance of the inner world of fundamental consciousness, will flee in horror and panic at the awesome power of the unfettered mind once it is free of the limitations of a body. If the compassion of the guide is strong, however, this fleeting period of transition between one lifetime and the next may be utilized as a great opportunity for permanent release from bondage. It is an opportunity to enter the state of total freedom so that the deceased person need never again be trapped in the miserable prison of rebirth and death.

Inspiring him or her with sincere regret concerning the futility of endlessly wandering around and around the cycle of existence, the guide should encourage the deceased person to renounce all attachment to the world and to turn his or her mind toward blissful liberation.

THE HORRORS

If you have not recognized any of these beings, both peaceful and fearsome, for what they are, you will become afraid of them and flee, only to experience yet more suffering.

If you fail to recognize them, then you will see the whole group of blood-drinking Herukas as Lords of Death. You will fear them, panic, and faint in terror. Your own projections will become demons and you will wander lost in the cycle of existence. No matter what terrifying things you see, recognize them as your own projections!

If you can do this, you will definitely become a buddha right now!

If you do not recognize your own projections for what they are, then they will arise as enormous, terrifying demons, Lords of Death, filling the entire universe around you, shrieking threats, tearing bodies apart, sucking up brains, and ripping out hearts and guts.

But remember that you have an astral body and cannot be really harmed by them. These demons also are actually devoid of any substantial existence, for they merely arise from the creative energy of your primordial mind.

Think of them as your spiritual friends and protectors come to guide you through the dangers of the transitional phase and all your fears will dissipate. At this time you should also pray with intense devotion to the Lord of Compassion or any other spiritual being with whom you have a connection. This is very important, for, if you do so, all your terror will leave you and you will certainly become a transfigured celestial buddha.

commentary

Until now, the text has described a journey of opportunities. If the deceased person has reached this stage and still has not seen the true nature of the experiences he or she has encountered, then these are lost chances. In terms of our own lives, the text has shown us how reality and our own intrinsic enlightenment are always present. First we are confronted with the bare primordial nature of our minds, free from all artifices and projections. Failing to recognize this, we gradually begin to drift away from this core of our being. Yet our inner wisdom tries to help us in the forms of images representing kind, peaceful beings, who are simply facets of our own enlightenment. If we still fail to recognize what we truly are, then the forces of our ego-mind begin to taint the experiences. All our negative emotions gradually emerge, each one carrying with it the danger of a negative lifestyle. By the end of this process, the elements of the ego-mind are all present.

If we have still failed to put any spiritual teachings into practice, the ego-mind drops into a state of total paranoia and disintegration, with each element turning into terrifying and hostile projections.

If this happens during our lifetimes, we become extremely defensive and hostile to the world around us. If this is experienced after death, then the ego projections take on the forms of ferocious demons and hostile beings. It is, therefore, very important for the guide at this stage to reassure the deceased person and to try and calm him or her, with a reminder that even these terrifying visions are no more than his or her own deluded projections.

THE TRANSITIONAL PHASE OF REBIRTH

❋

THE GOAL OF THE BUDDHIST PATH *is enlightenment and liberation from the cycle of repeated births and deaths. The Tibetans use pictorial means to convey profound teachings so that they may have greater impact. One such picture depicts the Wheel of Life, showing the various elements and phases of the cycle of life and rebirth. We are all subject to certain root psychological or emotional defects that drive us on through life after life. These are ignorance, symbolized by a cockerel; greedy attachment, shown as a pig; and hatred or anger, depicted as a snake. These motivational forces determine the moral quality of our actions and the spiritual residue of these actions is said to determine the manner of our rebirth.*

The outer rim of the Wheel features small pictures that illustrate the twelve interdependent causal phases involved in all experience. Ignorance is shown as a blind man, karmic formations as a potter, habitual propensities as a monkey playing with a peach, consciousness as two men in a boat, the six sense organs as six empty houses, contact between the senses and their objects as a couple making love, feeling as a man with an arrow in each eye, craving as a man drinking, attachment as a monkey snatching fruit, existence as a pregnant woman, birth as a woman in labor, and finally old age and death as a corpse. The whole wheel is held firmly in the jaws of the Lord of Death to remind us of our mortality.

114

THE TRANSITIONAL PHASE OF REBIRTH

ALTHOUGH THE GUIDE has already instructed the deceased person many times about the reality transitional phase, only those who previously had considerable experience of spiritual practice and who have positive karmic influences were able to recognize it. It is difficult for those who are afraid and have negative influences, who have little spiritual experience or who are very sinful. Therefore, the guide should instruct the deceased person in the following manner from around the thirteenth day onwards:

Listen carefully. [Name], and keep these instructions in mind! When the peaceful and wrathful deities appeared to you during the reality transitional phase, you did not recognize them for what they are and you fainted away. When you came to, your awareness became more lucid and you immediately saw yourself with an astral body similar in appearance to that you previously had. At this time do not chase after any of the projections that may arise for you now; do not become attached to them or hanker after them! If you do, then you will wander lost in the six realms of existence in misery.

Having an astral body such as this, you will come upon your relatives and your home as though in a dream. Though you try to talk to your relatives, they will not answer you. Seeing your relatives and loved ones weeping, you will think to yourself, "I am dead. What am I to do?" You will experience terrible anguish, like a fish twitching on hot sand. But it will not help you to torment yourself thus. If you have had a spiritual guide,

you should now pray to him or her. Or else, pray to whatever compassionate manifestation of spiritual energy you are familiar with.

It is useless now for you to cling longingly to your relatives and friends: let go of them! You will call out to the mourners, "Here I am! Don't cry!" But they will ignore you and then you will realize in anguish that you have indeed died. All around you there is a murky haze, like the gray of an autumn sky at dawn.

This phase will last for around twenty days according to your karmic influences. So pray to the Lord of Compassion and you will not experience anguish and fear.

commentary

After having been presented with so many chances for recognition and liberation, but not using them, people who are unfamiliar with the structure and working of their minds have no alternative but to move on to a new phase of experience. Whether during the death experience or on a subtle level during our own lifetimes, we are constantly presented with situations where our ego-self strives to recreate a comfortable and secure home for itself. The ego always tries to take the easy route to happiness, but any apparent benefits it achieves are illusory.

The challenge facing the deceased person at this stage is to try and find any possible avenues of liberation that still exist and to overcome the temptation to slip back into his or her normal lifestyle.

*During this time you will be beset by many terrors:
the feeling that you are being chased by demons,
carnivorous animals, and you will hear the
fearsome sounds of avalanches, floods, fires,
and hurricanes.*

*You may seem to gain shelter for a brief moment
by bridges, shrines or in huts and churches,
but you will not be able to stay for long.
Since your mind is now disembodied, it moves
about restlessly. You may feel cold, angry and
mentally unbalanced.*

*Then you will remember that you are dead
and wonder what you should do now.
You will feel intense unbounded misery.*

*Seeing your home, your friends and loved ones and
even your own corpse, you will think to yourself,
"What am I to do, now that I am dead?"
Your astral body will feel a great, crushing grief.
Then you may think of regaining a physical
body, so you will experience yourself searching
everywhere for a suitable body.*

*You may even try repeatedly to re-enter your own
corpse, but without success, since some time has
already elapsed while you were been in the reality
phase. In winter, your corpse will be frozen stiff,
while in summer, it will have begun to rot.
Or else your relatives have already cremated or
buried your body. Grief-stricken, you will feel as
though you are being squeezed between rocks and
stones. Such torments are characteristic of the
rebirth phase: though you search for a body, you
cannot escape this suffering. Stop all your efforts
to acquire a body and rest your mind without
distraction in the natural state of being that is
beyond action!*

commentary

We are afraid of spiritual development because it obliges us to examine our dearly held beliefs and the comforting structures that the ego-self has so carefully built to cocoon itself from change. Whenever we are challenged by problems in life or meet with any kind of profound crisis in our dealings with the world, our usual response is to try and recreate a safe mental environment identical to the one to which we were accustomed in the past.

After death, this response takes the form of trying to find ways of reanimating one's beloved body or, failing that, to find shelter in any place that seems to offer some comfort. But as the text points out, this is impossible. Similarly, during our own lifetimes, we can never truly return to the way we were before we met with any profound crisis or conflict. We must move on, but it is up to us whether we do so in a wholesome and liberating manner or just create more of the same.

If we have a teacher during our lifetime, we can turn to him or her for guidance and assistance. After death, it is vital that the guide should do whatever is in his or her power to lead the deceased person's consciousness to higher states. Even when the strength of negative actions overwhelms them with fear, and liberation is beyond their reach, the guide should continue to encourage and uplift them with every thought, word, and gesture.

IF THE GUIDE instructs the deceased person in this way, it is almost certain that he will be liberated from the rebirth phase. Yet if it is possible that the deceased has failed to recognize things as they are due to his negative karmic influences, the guide should call him once again thus:

Listen carefully, {Name}! The misery and suffering you are now experiencing is due to your own negative acts in the past, so you cannot blame anybody else! Pray devoutly to whatever embodiments of spiritual ideals you believe in and they will protect you. If you do not do this and do not know any other useful spiritual practices, then you will see your good and evil deeds being counted out like black and white pebbles. You will probably become very scared and irritated. You will tremble and try to lie to the Lord of Death who stands in judgment over you.

All your past deeds will suddenly be revealed to you, both good and evil, and you will know that your lies have been useless.

Then the Lord of Death will seize you with a rope around your neck and drag you away. He will chop off your head, rip out your heart, pull out your guts, suck your blood, and chew your flesh and bones. Yet despite the agony you will experience, you cannot really die even though you see your body being chopped up over and over again. So do not lie and do not be afraid of the Lord of Death!

If you can recognize all these things as hallucinatory projections that arise through your past karma, pray to whatever spiritual beings that give you comfort, call out to the Lord of Compassion and you will be liberated from rebirth. Abandon all your fears and anxieties!

commentary

Now the process of death is complete, and if the deceased person has not been liberated during this period, they will shortly be compelled by the force of negative deeds to re-enter the world. Thus those who care for the dead should now try to help them secure a good rebirth, while continually urging them toward their own liberation.

Yet, as is often the case, people emerge from the various upheavals in their lives without having truly learnt their significance. But while self-reflection is very important for spiritual growth, we are also in danger of recriminating and tormenting ourselves with pangs of guilt at our failures. In many religions, it is said that the dead are confronted with their own negative acts by some kind of judge who then punishes them for these misdeeds. However, this text teaches that even such judges are projections of the ego-mind. Here, the dead are aware of their own failings and stand in judgment over themselves. They are then in danger of tormenting themselves needlessly for their past deeds, when all that they should do is to renounce such negativity and attempt to cultivate the positive virtues to avoid evil acts in the future.

BUT EVEN THOUGH the guide explains all this many times to the deceased person, it is possible that he will still not be liberated from the rebirth phase because of many negative influences. The guide should once again call out to the deceased person:

Listen carefully, [Name]! If you have failed to recognize anything that has been explained to you, the memory of your past body will gradually fade and the appearance of your future one will become clearer. You will start looking for any body in which to be reborn. You will now feel drawn to anything that appears before you.

The six lights of the six realms of existence will gradually shine forth and the light of the realm most appropriate for your karmic past will shine brightest. These are the soft white light associated with the realm of the gods, the red of the demi-gods, the blue of humans, the green of animals, the yellow of the hungry ghosts, and the smoky light of the hell realms. At this moment, your astral body also takes on the color of the realm into which you are going to be reborn.

The key point of the instructions at this point is this: no matter which color shines before you, visualize that as the Lord of Compassion himself. Focus your mind intensely upon this image and gradually let it shrink and disappear into the empty luminosity of reality. You will then be liberated from all rebirths.

commentary

If the dead person fails to reform his or her actions and intentions, then the accumulated energy of repeated negative patterns of behavior will resurface and project them into the situations and lifestyles that are most suited to such patterns. Thus, excessive pride will lead them to seek the paradisical life of comfort and luxury that is symbolized by the realm of the gods. Jealousy and envy inevitably lead to a life of strife and conflict, symbolized by the warring demi-gods. Lust and attachment are traditionally thought to be typical of the ordinary human state. Dull stupidity and lack of awareness will result in the deceased returning to lead an animal-like life with few thoughts beyond eating, sleeping and sex. If the dead person is dominated by greed and avarice, he or she will become a dissatisfied miser who resembles the traditional hungry ghosts who never achieve any satisfaction. Finally, a life characterized by anger, malice, and hatred will lead to the anguish of paranoia that is symbolized by the hell realms.

It is important for us to recognize the negative emotion that predominates our personality during our lifetime, for then we can take steps to avoid falling into situations that merely serve to strengthen such negativity. If we truly feel unable to help ourselves, we can usefully turn to prayer, and ask for help from the divine compassion that shines out from enlightenment.

BLOCKING OFF ENTRANCE INTO A WOMB

❁

YET THESE INSTRUCTIONS will not be understood by one whose previous spiritual practice was shallow and inadequate. It is vital for the guide to give the deceased person the following instructions for blocking off entrance into a womb, for he will still be confused and will now stray to the entrance of a womb. The guide should call the deceased person thus:

Listen carefully, [Name]! If you have not understood the instructions you have already been given, you will now begin to have the sensation of moving upwards, sidewards or downwards through the power of your previous karmic acts. As previously

explained, you will also have visions of fierce winds, blizzards, hailstorms, and dark fogs, or of being pursued by crowds of people.

You will try to find a refuge and escape from them. At this time, you should bring to mind and visualize the Lord of Great Compassion or any other embodiment of your spiritual ideal. When you have a clear and vivid image of him before you, visualize him gradually dissolving inwards from the edges until nothing remains but the empty luminosity that is beyond conceptual thought. As you enter into this state, you will succeed in blocking off entrance into a womb.

commentary

The text now describes a number of techniques that can prevent people from falling back into old outworn modes of being. These techniques are the same whether they are put into practice by the living or the dead. The text reminds us that all of our experiences are products of our previous actions and habitual tendencies. The way we experience things, whether dead or alive, is dependent upon such accumulated energy.

One simple way to overcome our negative tendencies, when we do not have the spiritual training to apply more advanced methods, is to visualize the Lord of Compassion. The Lord of Compassion can take any form that is culturally appropriate to us, but the effect of relying on such a savior is always the same. If we try to focus on any image that embodies this religious ideal for us, we can identify ourselves with that goodness and thus be prevented from falling back into negative modes of life. The image of such a being acts as a conduit back to our own primordially enlightened mind that we never knew we had. If we can do this successfully, then by moving beyond the confines of our ego-mind, we can bypass all our negative deeds and intentions and gain liberation from their effects.

If this has not worked for you and you are on the brink of entering into a womb, there are still several ways of blocking off entrance into a womb. Concentrate and listen carefully!

You will now see couples making love. When you see them, do not enter in between them but hold yourself off with mindfulness. Instead see them as the divine Father and Mother and imagine yourself respectfully making offerings to them and asking them for their blessings. At this moment, you will definitely block off entrance to a womb.

If this fails to block off entrance to a womb and you are still on the verge of entering a womb, visualize the couple as the Lord of Compassion and his consort. Imagine yourself respectfully making offerings to them and devoutly ask them to bestow spiritual attainments upon you. This method will also block off entrance to a womb.

If this also fails to block off entrance to a womb and you are still on the verge of entering a womb, you can still do so by dispelling attachment and hatred. When you see couples making love, you will have strong feelings of jealousy. If you are going to be reborn as a male, you will feel desire for the woman and hatred for the man; if you are going to be reborn as a female, you will feel desire for the man and hatred for the woman.

When attachment and hatred arise in this way, you should say to yourself, "Alas! I have accumulated such negative karma that I have wandered lost in the cycle of existence until now because of attachment and hatred. If I continue to feel attachment and hatred in this way, I shall wander lost in the cycle of existence endlessly and sink again into the deep ocean of suffering. I resolve that I shall now abandon all attachment and hatred, never again to feel desire or aversion!" If you concentrate whole-heartedly on this thought, you will be able to block off entrance to a womb.

commentary

At this point, the text instructs us about the specific negative emotions that cause us to attempt a recreation of our familiar worlds. Though it talks in terms of a dead person seeking rebirth, it also implicitly shows us the factors that cause us to repeat negative behavior patterns during our own lifetimes.

Our ego-mind adopts various strategies to ensure its survival. Its chief tools are the negative emotions of attachment and aversion. When we encounter a new and unfamiliar situation, we generally make some kind of value judgment about it so that we can safely deal with it. In this way, the ego-mind protects itself from change. Sometimes we find the situation comforting to the ego's sense of self-importance. In such cases, we attempt to incorporate the situation or experience into ourselves by attachment and clinging. At other times, our ego-mind finds itself threatened by what it finds, so we then tend to reject that situation with loathing and hatred.

However, it is these two negative emotions – attachment and aversion – that are the chief building blocks of all our misfortune. For though our ego-mind adopts these strategies, they ultimately fail and lead to more dissatisfaction and unhappiness. We forget that it is an intrinsic fact of existence that all things change, and we cannot hold onto any cherished modes of life and behavior without disappointment.

*B*ut even if you have done this and yet it has failed to block off entrance to a womb and you are still on the verge of entering a womb, then you can still do so by meditating on the unreal nature of things. You should tell yourself that all you are experiencing is illusory: the father, the mother, the impelling force of your karmic acts. Though they appear to you, they are in fact unreal. They are like mirages or images in dreams. All these things are merely projections of your mind's own making. If you can shatter your belief in their reality in this way, then you will be able to block off entrance to a womb.

commentary

The text now teaches another technique to avoid falling back into negative lifestyles. Although our psychological world and the people around us seem solid and real, this is not the case. All phenomena we experience are subject to change and impermanence, and they are all also products of projections that the ego-mind has generated. Seen in this way, the things that we experience, whether they attract or repel us, are quite insubstantial. When a stage-hypnotist has worked his skills upon us, we may believe in the reality of whatever is suggested to us and act accordingly. We may be told that a cold rod of iron is a red-hot poker and when touched by it our skin bubbles up in blisters. But the audience can see that there is no hot iron present, though the subject believes otherwise. The subject has been convinced that an illusion is real. It is the same for us in the wider world of experience. Our ego-selves are the skilled magicians that create illusory experiences that seem real until we understand how we have been fooled by their projections. When we see through their apparent reality and false substantiality, they crumble away and cease to have any hold on us.

CHOOSING A SUITABLE WOMB

YET THERE ARE SOME who had very little experience of virtuous behavior but steeped themselves in negative acts throughout their lives. Because of many negative tendencies they will not be freed even yet, even though they have been given these instructions and help over and over again. So now the deceased person should be taught the method to choose a suitable womb in case he has not been able to block his entrance into a womb. The guide should call on the deceased person thus:

Listen carefully, [Name]! Even though you have already been given instructions many times, you have not understood them. Since you have not blocked the womb entrance, it is now time for you to take on a new body. Listen carefully and keep the instructions in mind!

You will begin to see various signs which indicate the place and condition of your future rebirth. Some places will appear very alluring while others may seem disgusting. No matter what places appear to your clairvoyant sight, do not go to them but generate the urge to resist their attraction and the illusion of safety they give you! If you have previously learned any special spiritual practices, remember them now and use them to block your entry into a womb. If nothing else, try to visualize the Lord of Compassion and be drawn to him. In this way you will become a transfigured celestial buddha.

commentary

If we have not developed sufficiently in our spiritual lives and lack the insight to take advantage of the previous teachings, then there are still other ways that we can help ourselves. Our ego-minds often play tricks on us because of our propensity for particular lifestyles. Though we may rationally be aware that a particular mode of behavior is unwholesome and will lead to unhappiness, our egos convince us that such lifestyles are attractive and pleasant though in fact they are likely to be nothing of the sort. Similarly, the ego will want to avoid future situations that threaten its security, and so will tell you that another course of action is unpleasant and to be avoided.

Because of our pervasive spiritual immaturity, we are often unable to see things in their true light. We have no guarantee that any situation is really what our ego tells us it is. In such cases, it is best to adopt a mode of equanimity and accept whatever life offers us without indulging in value judgments.

IF IT IS LIKELY that the deceased person has still failed to free himself from the cycle of existence in that way, the guide should now instruct him as follows:

If this has failed, you should use your clairvoyant powers to choose a suitable womb in the best of places in the human realm. Your future mother should at least live in a place where advanced spiritual teachings are widespread. Before you enter her womb, you should resolve to devote your future life to the practice of whatever is wholesome and will benefit others. This resolution is very important to ensure entry into a suitable womb.

Yet, in choosing a womb, it is possible to make a mistake because of the influence of your previous karmic acts: you may see a suitable womb as bad or a bad womb as suitable. It is very important at this point to view such potential wombs in a spirit of detachment. Even if a womb appears to be suitable, do not view it with grasping; if a womb appears to be bad, do not view it with aversion.

commentary

In passing through the transitional phase of death, the dead have now almost run out of options, even though they have had many opportunities presented to them from the depths of their own spiritual being that could have freed them from their negative tendencies.

In life, also, we might not be able to make any real progress toward freedom. It is possible that our circumstances make it impossible at present for us to engage in any sort of activities that bring about spiritual growth. In such situations, we can at least resolve to change some elements of our situation so that it is more conducive to spiritual health.

We might find it is advantageous to drop out of the rat-race and take up a more peaceful occupation. Similarly, we might find ourselves locked in destructive relationships with other people. If we cannot change ourselves directly, we can at least try to eliminate the more obvious obstacles in our lives. In this way we can create a little space for ourselves, and then we may find the time and energy to devote ourselves to what really matters, spiritual practice.

HOWEVER, UNLESS THE deceased has had some experience in cultivating detachment in the past, it will be quite difficult for him to free himself from the disease of negative tendencies. If the deceased cannot rid himself of attachment or hatred, he can free himself from such negativity by asking the representatives of his highest spiritual ideals to protect him, even though he is extremely stupid, sinful, and animal-like. The guide should once again call the deceased person thus:

Listen [Name]! If you do know how to choose a suitable womb for rebirth and yet cannot abandon attachment or hatred, you should call on the representatives of your highest spiritual ideals and ask them to protect you, regardless of whatever you experience at this time. Pray to the Lord of Compassion! Hold your head up high and move on! Give up all clinging attachment to your relatives and friends! Go now into the blue light of the human realm or else the white light of the divine realm!

commentary

If all else has failed for the deceased person, the text shows that they have one final chance to better themselves by choosing an environment that offers some security and hope for the future.

During our lives, when we are so overwhelmed by our negative attachment and aversion, there may be little we can do for ourselves. At such times, we should turn to more conventional and less demanding forms of religion. If we do not have the time and inclination to devote ourselves to the regular practice of meditation, we can at least open ourselves up a little through the humility of prayer.

We can adopt simple forms of religious practice. Instead of living with attachment and greed, we can try to become a little more generous and giving toward others. We can make efforts to treat people with some kindness and dignity rather than with the normal hostility and aggression we indulge in. When we pray for help from higher spiritual beings with humility, at least we have begun to recognize our own limitations and need for change. In this sense, even the most basic religious practices have some value, no matter how naive they may seem to us.

The *Great Liberation through Hearing* is a means to assist many types of spiritual practitioners gain liberation during the transitional phases of dying and death. Those of the highest ability will be able to liberate themselves at the moment of death and completely bypass these transitional phases. Those of medium ability with some experience of meditation will recognize the radiant luminosity that appears at the moment of death and thereby be liberated. Those of lesser ability will be able to recognize the various visions of the peaceful and wrathful deities in the reality transitional phase during the following days. Those with no religious training, and those who have many negative karmic tendencies, wander on into the transitional phase of rebirth, but they can block off their entry into a womb and thereby be released from the cycle of existence. Even the lowest types of people who are bestial and burdened with heavy sins can be turned away from miserable states of rebirth and gain a human body, enabling them to embark on a life of virtue and spiritual training in their next incarnation.

Hence, the guide should try to assist all those who have died. If the body of the deceased person is present, the guide should read these instructions over and over again until blood and lymph trickles from the nostrils of the corpse. Until then, the corpse should not be moved or disturbed by mourning relatives and friends.

It is also very beneficial if you read and study these instructions during your own lifetime and try to learn it all by heart. If you do not forget its words even though you were to be chased by seven wild dogs, you will definitely be able to achieve liberation during the transitional phases of dying and death.

•

The *Great Liberation through Hearing during the Transitional Phases of Dying and Death* is completed. May it be of benefit to all who read it!

GLOSSARY

All-good Father (Samantabhadra) The male embodiment of the radiant energy aspect of primordial awareness and ultimate reality, who is also the primordial source of all the buddhas. Also Samantabhadra, one of the eight bodhisattva attendants who appear during the peaceful visions.

All-good Mother (Samantabhadri) The female embodiment of the unformed matrix aspect of primordial awareness and ultimate reality.

Animals One of the six modes of existence or experience, characterized emotionally by ignorance.

Archetypal deity (Yi-dam) An embodiment of Enlightenment with whom one has a particular affinity and who provides a template for one's spiritual growth during meditation.

Astral body A non-material body formed by mental energy and which arise during dreaming, during the death phase or during meditation.

Bodhisattva A spiritually advanced being who aspires for Enlightenment in order to benefit all beings and whose particular type of activities are linked to their path of development.

Buddha-realm Any one of the numerous places throughout the universe which are created by Buddhas and provide ideal conditions for the spiritual advancement of those reborn there through their faith and virtue.

Clear light The manner in which the inherent energy of reality or primordial awareness appears initially to a dead person. This experience can also be cultivated through meditation during life.

Continuum of reality The totality of reality in which its pure absolute aspect as emptiness and its impure relative aspect as everyday phenomena are indivisible.

Cycle of existence The repeated cycle of births and deaths experienced by unenlightened beings due to the effects of their karmic actions, which comprises six modes of existence or experience: as a god, a demi-god, a human, an animal, a hungry ghost, or a hell-being.

Dakini Female spiritual beings, usually somewhat fearsome in appearance, who assist and protect those on the Buddhist path.

Demi-gods One of the six modes of existence or experience who are characterized emotionally by jealousy and envy.

Ego-self A construct of the unenlightened mind, believed by the individual to be real and permanent, and which acts as a focal point for generally negative emotions and actions.

Elements The basic forces which generate relative material existence, symbolized by earth, water, fire, wind and space, and which provide, respectively, solidity, cohesion, warmth, movement, and location.

Emptiness The real nature of things in that they are devoid of inherent existence. This is also one aspect of primordial reality and awareness, symbolized by the All-good Mother.

Enlightenment The perfection of all good qualities and the complete elimination of all negative emotions and karmic traces realized when one becomes a Buddha.

Garuda An eagle-like mythical bird.

Goddess One of the eight embodiments of offerings who are the companions of the eight bodhisattvas appearing during the peaceful visions.

Gods One of the six modes of existence or experience who are characterized emotionally by pride.

Grasping Attachment to existence arising from the ego-self's belief in its reality and permanence.

Habitual memory patterns The mental imprints of thoughts, emotions and actions. These are generally negative in quality and provide the energy for continued cyclical existence.

Hell beings One of the six modes of existence or experience, characterized emotionally by anger and hatred.

Hero The male counterpart of a *dakini.*

Heruka Literally "blood-drinker," these are the wrathful male manifestations of enlightenment who assist those particularly afflicted by negativity and non-virtuous deeds.

Humans One of the six modes of existence or experience, characterized emotionally by attachment and lust.

Hungry ghosts One of the six modes of existence or experience, characterized emotionally by avarice and greed.

Initiation Also known as "empowerment," this is the ritual bestowal by a tantric master of the power and authorization needed to embark on advanced tantric practices.

Karma The process by which the cycle of births and deaths is maintained. Karma is traditionally defined as a person's motivations or intentions and the acts to which they give rise. These are generally negative although they can also be positive in a limited way.

Mandala The universe as the idealized spiritual realm of the Buddhas and their entourage, and also the limited graphic representation of that.

Mantra Special words or sounds associated with the speech faculty of Buddhas. These can be used for protection, purification and as meditational aids.

Meditation The cultivation of mental peace and insight. Advanced meditation using tantric techniques involve the extensive use of visualization and mantras.

Negative emotions The six basic negative strategies that the ego-self adopts to preserve its illusion of existence – stupidity, attachment, hatred, jealousy, pride, and opinionatedness – as well as the mass of subsidiary emotions deriving from these six.

Primordial mind The aspect of intrinsic reality which is endowed with awareness. This is also a term for a person's own inherent but concealed enlightenment.

Projections The deluded and unenlightened mind superimposes its own distorted pseudo-reality upon whatever is experienced through the power of habitual tendencies.

Radiant luminosity Same as the Clear light.

Transfigured celestial Buddha The manner in which an enlightened being or Buddha manifests to advanced people. This term also includes all the Buddhas in their peaceful and wrathful forms that appear after death.

Vajra A ritual implement with five or nine prongs at each end which symbolizes the indestructible power and cohesion of Enlightenment.

Vidyadhara A realized tantric master, both on human and on archetypal levels.

Visualization The meditational process of generating an image of a particular enlightened being or archetype with whom one identifies oneself in order to awaken similar qualities within oneself.

SUGGESTED READING LIST

Avedon, John F. 1984.
In Exile from the Land of the Snows.
Knopf.

Avedon, John F. 1988.
Tibet Today: Current Conditions & Prospects.
Wisdom Publications.

Batchelor, Stephen. 1994.
The Awakening of the West.
Aquarian.

Bernbaum, Edwin. 1980.
The Way to Shambhala.
Doubleday.

Beyer, Stephan. 1973.
The Cult of Tara. Magic and Ritual in Tibet.
University of California Press.

Brauen, Martin. 1997.
The Mandala.
London: Serindia Publications.

Byrom, T. 1993.
The Dhammapada.
Shambhala Publications.

Cabezon, Jose Ignacio Ed. 1996.
Tibetan Literature.
Snow Lion.

Chang, Garma. 1977.
The Six Yogas of Naropa.
Snow Lion.

Dowman, Keith. 1997.
The Sacred Life of Tibet.
Thorsons.

Farrer-Halls, Gill. 1998.
The World of the Dalai Lama.
Thorsons.

Freke, Timothy. 1998.
The Wisdom of the Tibetan Lamas.
Godsfield Press.

Fremantle, Francesca & Chogyam Trungpa. 1975.
The Tibetan Book of the Dead.
Shambhala Publications.

Guenther, Herbert. 1972.
Buddhist Philosophy in Theory and Practice.
Shambhala Publications.

Gyatso, Tenzin, H.H. the Dalai Lama. 1984. *Kindness, Clarity and Insight.*
Snow Lion.

Gyatso, Tenzin, H.H. the Dalai Lama. 1991.
MindScience: An East-West Dialogue.
Snow Lion.

Gyatso, Tenzin, H.H. the Dalai Lama. 1997.
Healing Anger. Snow Lion.

Kalu Rinpoche. 1986.
The Dharma that illuminates all beings impartially like the light of the Sun and Moon.
State University of New York Press.

Kalu Rinpoche. 1997.
Luminous Mind.
Wisdom Publications.

Levine, Norma. 1996.
A Yearbook of Buddhist Wisdom.
Godsfield Press.

Lhalungpa, Lobsang. 1996.
Life of Milarepa.
Shambhala Publications.

Norbu, Thubten Jigme. 1972.
Tibet. Its History, Religion and People.
Penguin Books.

Nyi-ma Rinpoche, Chokyi. 1991.
The Bardo Guidebook. Kathmandu:
Rangjung Yeshe.

Rabten, Geshe. 1988.
Treasury of the Dharma:
A Tibetan Buddhist Meditation Course.
Tharpa Publications.

Rangdrol, Tsele Natsok. 1989.
The Mirror of Mindfulness.
Shambhala Publications.

Reynolds, John M. 1996.
The Golden Letters.
Snow Lion Publications.

Saddhatissa, H. 1997.
Buddhist Ethics.
Wisdom Publications.

Shakabpa, W. D. 1967.
Tibet: A Political History.
Yale University Press.

Snellgrove, David. 1987.
Indo-Tibetan Buddhism.
Shambhala Publications.

Sogyal Rinpoche. 1992.
The Tibetan Book of Living and Dying.
HarperCollins.

Tarthang Tulku. 1978.
Openness Mind.
Dharma Publishing.

Tarthang Tulku. 1978.
Skillful Means.
Dharma Publishing.

Trungpa, Chogyam. 1974.
Cutting through Spiritual Materialism.
Shambhala Publications.

Trungpa, Chogyam. 1976.
The Myth of Freedom.
Shambhala Publications.

Thurman, Robert. 1994.
The Tibetan Book of the Dead.
Bantam Books (US) and Thorsons.

Wallace, Vesna and B. Alan. 1997.
A Guide to the Bodhisattva
Way of Life.
Snow Lion.

USEFUL ADDRESSES

RIGPA UK
330 Caledonian Road
London N1 1BB
UK
tel: (0171) 7000185 *after 2.30pm GMT*

SPIRIT ROCK
Meditation Center
PO Box 909
Woddacre CA 94973
USA

YUNGDRUNG BON STUDY CENTER
c/o Flat G2, 216 Berkeley Street
Glasgow G3 7HQ
Scotland
UK
tel: (0141) 226 5719

YUNGDRUNG BON STUDY CENTER
c/o Building 16,
The Lincolnsfield Center
Bushey Hall Drive
Bushey
Hertfordshire WD2 2ER
UK
tel: (01923) 228858 or (01923) 467965

BOOK SERVICES AND JOURNALS
WISDOM BOOKS
402 Hoe Street,
London E17 9AA
tel: (0181) 520 5588

WISDOM PUBLICATIONS
361 Newbury Street,
Boston MA 02115,
USA

BUDDHISM NOW
published by Buddhism
Publication Group,
Sharpham Coach Yard,
Ashprington,
Totnes,
Devon TQ9 7UT
UK

INQUIRING MIND
PO Box 9999
North Berkeley Station
Berkeley CA 94709
USA

THE MIDDLE WAY
published by The Buddhist Society
58 Eccleston Square
London SW1V 1PH
UK
tel: (0171) 834 5858 *between 2-6pm*
GMT only

SHAMBALA SUN
PO Box 399
Halifax, NS
Canada B3J 2P8
tel: 902 422-8404
fax: 902 423-2750

TRICYCLE, the Buddhist review
163 West 22nd Street
New York NY10011,
USA
tel: 212 645-1143
fax: 212 645-1493

ACKNOWLEDGMENTS

The Publishers are grateful to the following for permission to reproduce copyright material:

Eye Ubiquitous, Shoreham, Sussex:
Bennett Dean: pp. 9, 14, 19, 28, 35, 44, 45, 50, 52, 53, 62, 65, 76, 77, 78, 80, 82, 88, 91, 93, 104, 107, 125, 128, 129, 132, 134
Chris Gibb: p. 40
Adrian Girrou: p. 10
Tim Hawkins: p. 33
Sean Holmes: p. 61
L. Johnstone: p. 69
Tony Jones: p. 46
Bruce Low: p. 13
Sue Passmore: p. 30
Bryan Pickering: p. 32
Tim Page: pp. 67, 89
Damien Pet: p. 95
Pam Smith: p. 70
Julia Waterlow: pp. 2/3, 6/7, 8, 11, 12, 18, 20, 21, 24/35, 27, 34, 36, 37, 38/39, 42, 47, 48, 49, 55, 58, 59, 60, 64, 66, 71, 74/75, 79, 83, 86, 87, 90, 94, 96, 99, 101, 103, 105, 112, 113, 114, 116/117, 117, 118, 121, 123, 127, 130, 131, 136/137

James Davis Travel Photography, Shoreham, Sussex:
pp. 56/57, 75, 81, 84/85, 106, 119, 120, 126, 135

The Bridgeman Art Library/Oriental Museum Durham:
pp. 43, 114

The Stock Market, London: pp. 17, 23, 29, 31, 38, 41, 51, 54, 63, 97, 98, 10, 102, 108, 109, 110/111, 122/123, 124